D0050602

ESSENTIAL
PARIS

Original text by Elisabeth Morris

Revised and updated by Renata Rubnikowicz

© AA Media Limited 2011
First published 2007. Content verified and updated 2011
ISBN: 978-0-7495-6017-1

Published by AA Publishing, a trading name of AA Media Limited, whose registered office is Fanum House, Basing View, Basingstoke, Hampshire RG21 4EA. Registered number 06112600.

Colour separation: AA Digital Department
Printed and bound in Italy by Printer Trento S.r.l.

Find out more about AA Publishing and the wide range of services the AA provides by visiting our website at theAA.com/shop

A04193
Maps in this title produced from cartographic data © Tele Atlas N.V. 2010   Tele Atlas
© IGN France
Transport map © Communicarta Ltd, UK

About this book

Symbols are used to denote the following categories:

➕ map reference to maps on cover

✉ address or location

☎ telephone number

🕐 opening times

✋ admission charge

🍴 restaurant or café on premises
   or nearby

🚇 nearest underground train station

🚌 nearest bus/tram route

⛴ nearest ferry stop

🚃 nearest overground train station

✈ nearest airport

ℹ tourist information

❓ other practical information

▶ indicates the page where you will
   find a fuller description

This book is divided into six sections.

The essence of Paris pages 6–19
Introduction; Features; Food and drink;
Short break including the 10 Essentials

Planning pages 20–33
Before you go; Getting there; Getting
around; Being there

Best places to see pages 34–55
The unmissable highlights of any visit
to Paris

Best things to do pages 56–81
Great cafés; stunning views; places to
take the children and more

Exploring pages 82–165
The best places to visit in Paris,
organized by area

Excursions pages 166–183
Places to visit out of town

Maps
All map references are to the maps on
the covers. For example, Notre-Dame
has the reference ➕ 25Q – indicating
the grid square in which it can be found.

Admission prices
Inexpensive (under €6)
Moderate (€6–€10)
Expensive (over €10)

Hotel prices
Price are per room per night:
€ budget (under €100);
€€ moderate (€100–€200);
€€€ expensive to luxury (over €200)

Restaurant prices
Price for a three-course meal per person
without drinks:
€ budget (under €30);
€€ moderate (€30–€75);
€€€ expensive (over €75)

Contents

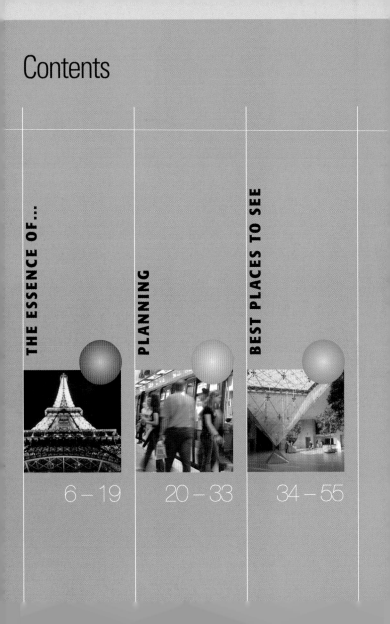

BEST THINGS TO DO

EXPLORING...

EXCURSIONS

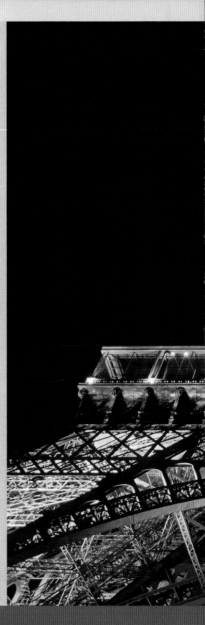

The essence of...

Paris is order, harmony, beauty and elegance – the result of bold town planning that successfully married tradition and innovation, sometimes with stunning effects. You see it in the exclamation mark of the Eiffel Tower that pierces the city skyline and the stark glass pyramid erected in the heart of the Louvre.

Paris is also passion, youth, fine cuisine, fashion and a stimulating cultural life. Always renewing itself with new attractions and events while cherishing its heritage of art nouveau métro entrances and traditional pavement (sidewalk) cafés, the city of light earns its place as the world's most visited city.

features

Paris may seem straightforward and orderly to the first-time visitor viewing its wealth of stately monuments, but get to know it better and you will discover a complex city and find its beauty has many aspects. As well as sweeping vistas and grand squares and boulevards, it is made up of picturesque villages such as Saint-Germain-des-Prés, the Marais and Montmartre, whose tiny, half-hidden squares and twisting streets are steeped in romantic atmosphere, and where you may unexpectedly come upon a bold modern sculpture defiantly competing with a medieval masterpiece. However, an overall sense of harmony prevails.

The pace of life is notoriously hectic in this compact, densely populated city. Fortunately, there are plenty of quiet spots, full of charm and mystery, ideal for relaxing after a head-spinning shopping spree in boulevard Haussmann or a marathon session in the Louvre.

GEOGRAPHY

● Situated in the heart of northern France, some 250km (155 miles) from the sea, Paris lies on the banks of the meandering river Seine.

THE CITY
● The city is relatively small, entirely surrounded by the *boulevard périphérique*, an often congested 35km-long (22-mile) ring road. Green spaces cover an area of 496ha (1,226 acres) excluding Bois de Boulogne and Bois de Vincennes and there is one tree for every four Parisians.

GREATER PARIS
● The surrounding area, known as the *banlieues*, includes densely populated suburbs, small towns and traditional villages scattered through the green belt, as well as several new towns. The region enjoys a reasonably dry climate, fairly cold in winter, hot and sunny in summer.

ADMINISTRATION
● Paris is a municipality administered by a council and a mayor like any other town in France, but it is also a *département* (county) headed by a *préfet*.
● Paris is divided into 20 *arrondissements* numbered from 1 to 20 starting from the Louvre in the historic centre.

POPULATION
● The city has just over 2 million inhabitants but nearly 11 million people, almost one-fifth of the French population, live in Greater Paris.

PARIS BY NUMBERS
● The 200 nationalities who live in Paris enjoy 20,000 cafés, 130 museums and 372 cinemas.
● The 13km (8 miles) of the river Seine that wind through the city are crossed by 37 bridges.
● Within the city boundaries lie 400 parks and gardens and 110 fountains.
● Streets are dotted with 80,000 lamp posts, 790 advertising columns and 9,300 public benches.

food & drink

In France, eating is an art that reaches its highest expression in Paris, for here the diversity and know-how of traditional regional cuisine are combined with a creative spirit stimulated by a strong cosmopolitan influence. In recent years, a growing awareness of the benefits of healthier living has seen many restaurants and produce markets promoting *bio* (organic) ingredients.

EATING PARISIAN STYLE

The traditional French breakfast of bread, butter and jam with a large cup of *café au lait* (white coffee) has largely given way to cereals and milk with tea (sometimes a *tisane* or herbal brew), hot chocolate or black coffee. The traditional croissants are often a weekend treat, when people breakfast *en famille*.

Most working people eat lunch in a café or restaurant. Once café and restaurant tables spread out onto the pavements only in spring and summer, but now that smoking is banned inside public establishments, smokers sit outside, often under heaters, all year round. Bustling waiters are continually calling out for *steak frites* (steak and fries) at the tops of their voices, as Parisians order their favourite lunchtime dish. Portions are adequate but not enormous, meaning that diners can manage three courses comfortably in an hour.

These days, when so many couples both work, dinner at home around 8pm may include a freshly prepared dish bought from a local *traiteur* (delicatessen) to save time, but will still probably begin with an hors-d'oeuvre, finish with cheese or dessert and be accompanied by a glass of wine.

SHOPPING FOR FOOD

Parisians are still very fond of their local street markets. There is one in almost every *quartier*, selling fruit and vegetables, cheese, *charcuterie* (sausages and cold meats), fish and meat. *Boulangeries* (bakers) stay open late and on Sundays, for *baguettes*, the traditional long, crusty loaves are as popular as ever.

EATING OUT

Parisian restaurants serve a wide choice of regional French dishes, though other cuisines are well represented. Seafood is popular; restaurants often display several varieties of *huitres* (oysters) to eat in or take away. In 2009, to boost restaurant trade, tax was lowered on food, but not on alcohol, so your bill will show two different rates of tax.

Even quite modest restaurants will stick strictly to traditional mealtimes. Look for the sign *"service continu"* which means that meals are served without interruption between lunch and dinner.

If you are on a budget lunch is your best option for trying different restaurants. Nearly all offer a

fixed-price menu at lunchtime. You can choose two or three courses from a list of *entrée et plat* (starter and main course), or *plat et dessert* (main course and dessert). Sometimes coffee and wine are included. There is usually a good-value *plat du jour* (dish of the day).

Other inexpensive refuelling options are a sweet or savoury *crêpe* (pancake) from a street stall (stand) or a *croque monsieur* (cheese on toast) from a café. *Boulangeries* sell filled baguettes.

WINE

In all but the finest restaurants you can order wine by the glass or by the *pichet* (carafe). These come in 25cl *(un quart)*, 50cl *(un demi)* and 75cl (equivalent to a bottle). There is often a list of *vins du mois* (wines of the month), which will be good value. A free carafe of tap water will usually be provided.

15

short break

If you have only a short time to visit Paris and would like to take home some unforgettable memories you can do something local and capture the real flavour of the city. The following suggestions will give you a wide range of sights and experiences that won't take very long, won't cost very much and will make your visit very special. If you only have time to choose just one of these, you will have found the true heart of the city.

● **Take a boat trip along the Seine** from the pont de l'Alma and admire the stately monuments whose splendour is dramatically enhanced at night by powerful floodlights. It's a great way to view some of the city's major sights from a different and magical perspective, and you can see many famous landmarks in just over an hour.

● **Climb to the top of the Tour Eiffel** for an aerial view of Paris (➤ 54–55); it's a guaranteed thrill from the panoramic lift (elevator). Visit early morning or late at night to avoid queues, but for the best views come an hour before sunset. You can get your postcards stamped with the famous Eiffel Tower postmark at the post office on level one.

● **Take a morning walk through the attractive Jardin du Luxembourg** and stand beside the romantic Fontaine de Médicis, named after Marie de Médicis, wife of Henri IV, who commissioned the Palais du Luxembourg (➤ 106).

● **Sit outside Les Deux Magots café** in boulevard St-Germain, on the Left Bank, and watch the world go by (➤ 59). This Paris institution, named after the wooden statues of two Chinese dignitaries *(magots)* inside the café, has managed to retain its literary feel. Street bustle peaks around lunchtime and from 6pm.

● **Stand on the pont de la Tournelle** near Notre Dame: look downriver for panoramic views of "old Paris" (Île de la Cité and beyond) and upriver for contrasting views of "new Paris" (Bercy and the Institut du Monde Arabe; ➤ 89).

● **Stroll along the *quais*** and browse through the *bouquinistes'* stock of old prints and books (➤ 50–51). These rickety old green booths are very much a part of the Parisian riverscape.

● **Take the funicular to Sacré-Coeur** at the top of Montmartre for stunning views of the city (➤ 52–53). It runs all day and costs one métro ticket each way.

● **Visit the *grands magasins*** (department stores) on boulevard Haussmann, even if you're not a shopper. Look up in Galeries Lafayette's (➤ 81) perfume hall to see its neo-Byzantine glass dome or enjoy lunch at Printemps' (➤ 80) rooftop cafeteria.

● **Stand on the place de la Concorde** at night and look along the Champs-Elysées (➤ 40–41). The illuminated avenue, gently rising towards the Arc de Triomphe, offers one of the most perfect urban vistas in the world. The 3,200-year-old obelisk at its centre is the city's most ancient monument.

● **Mingle with Parisians** doing their daily shopping in the street markets. In the Quartier Latin, the rue Mouffetard (➤ 99; closed Mondays) is typical, while on Sundays you can buy organic food *(bio)* in the market on boulevard Raspail.

Planning

Before you go

WHEN TO GO

JAN	FEB	MAR	APR	MAY	JUN	JUL	AUG	SEP	OCT	NOV	DEC
7°C	7°C	10°C	16°C	17°C	23°C	25°C	26°C	21°C	16°C	12°C	8°C
45°F	45°F	50°F	61°F	63°F	73°F	77°F	79°F	70°F	61°F	54°F	46°F

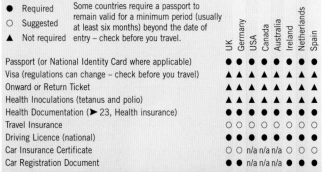

🟦 High season   ⬜ Low season

Temperatures are the average daily maximum for each month.

The best time to visit Paris is June, a glorious month when the days are longest, with the most sunshine and average daytime temperatures a comfortable 23°C (73°F). The city reaches peak tourist capacity in July. August sees the Parisian exodus to the countryside leaving the city emptier than usual. It is the hottest, most humid month and the city is prone to sudden storms.

September and October generally have a high percentage of crisp days and clear skies, but rooms can be difficult to find as this is the peak trade-fair period.

Winter temperatures rarely drop below freezing, but it rains frequently, sometimes with hail, from November to January.

WHAT YOU NEED

● Required
○ Suggested
▲ Not required

Some countries require a passport to remain valid for a minimum period (usually at least six months) beyond the date of entry – check before you travel.

	UK	Germany	USA	Canada	Australia	Ireland	Netherlands	Spain
Passport (or National Identity Card where applicable)	●	●	●	●	●	●	●	●
Visa (regulations can change – check before you travel)	▲	▲	▲	▲	▲	▲	▲	▲
Onward or Return Ticket	▲	▲	▲	▲	▲	▲	▲	▲
Health Inoculations (tetanus and polio)	▲	▲	▲	▲	▲	▲	▲	▲
Health Documentation (► 23, Health insurance)	●	●	●	●	●	●	●	●
Travel Insurance	○	○	○	○	○	○	○	○
Driving Licence (national)	●	●	●	●	●	●	●	●
Car Insurance Certificate	○	○	n/a	n/a	n/a	○	○	○
Car Registration Document	●	●	n/a	n/a	n/a	●	●	●

WEBSITES

Paris Tourist Office:
www.parisinfo.com
(this site also has information for
visitors with disabilities)

City of Paris:
www.paris.fr
French Tourist Office:
www.franceguide.com

TOURIST OFFICES AT HOME

In the UK French Government
Tourist Office, Lincoln House, 300
High Holborn, London WC1V 7JH
☎ 09068 244123

In Canada French Tourist Office
1800 avenue McGill, College Suite
1010, Montréal H3A 3J6
☎ 514/288-2026

In the USA French Tourist Office
825 Third Avenue, 29th Floor,

New York, NY10022
☎ 514/288-1904

French Government Tourist Office
9454 Wilshire Boulevard, Suite 210,
Beverly Hills, CA90212
☎ 514/288-1904

In Australia French Tourist Office
Level 13, 25 Bligh Street, Sydney,
NSW 2000
☎ (02) 9231 5244

HEALTH INSURANCE

Nationals of EU countries can obtain medical treatment at reduced cost
with the European Health Insurance Card (EHIC; www.ehic.org). Private
medical insurance is advised and is essential for other visitors.

Nationals of EU countries can also obtain dental treatment at reduced
cost. However, private medical insurance is advised for all visitors.

TIME DIFFERENCES

GMT	France	Spain	USA (NY)	USA (West Coast)	Sydney
12 noon	1pm	1pm	7am	4am	10pm

France is on Central European Time, one hour ahead of Greenwich Mean
Time (GMT +1). From late March, when clocks are put forward one hour,
until late October, French summer time (GMT +2) operates.

NATIONAL HOLIDAYS

1 Jan *New Year's Day*
Mar/Apr *Easter Monday*
1 May *May Day*
8 May *VE (Victory in Europe) Day*
6th Thu after Easter
Ascension Day

May/Jun *Whit Monday*
14 Jul *Bastille Day*
15 Aug *Assumption*
1 Nov *All Saints' Day*
11 Nov *Remembrance Day*
25 Dec *Christmas Day*

Banks, businesses, museums and most shops (except boulangeries) are closed on these days.

WHAT'S ON WHEN

The events listed here are liable to change from one year to the next and sometimes have more than one venue. Dates may also vary slightly.

PARIS

February *Carnaval de Paris:* A fancy-dress parade winds through Belleville and place de la République to Hôtel de Ville. www.carnavaldeparis.org

April *Paris Marathon:* Thousands of runners start from the Champs-Élysées. www.parismarathon.com

May *Jazz at Saint-Germain-des-Prés:* International artists play in the church and nearby venues in a two-week festival. www.parisinfo.com

June *Fête de la Musique:* On 21 June squares, gardens and streets come alive in a free music festival. www.fetedelamusique.culture.fr

Gay Pride: Outrageously dressed participants parade between Montparnasse and place de la Bastille. www.gaypride.fr

June–July *Paris Jazz Festival:* Open-air concerts in the Parc Floral de Paris, Bois de Vincennes. www.parisjazzfestival.net

Festival Chopin: A tribute to the Romantic composer at the Orangerie de Bagatelle in the heart of the Bois de Boulogne. www.frederic-chopin.com

July *Tour de France:* The world's premier bicycle event arrives in the city and riders race for the finish down the Champs-Élysées. www.letour.fr

14 July *Bastille Day:* France's National Day is celebrated with military parades along the Champs-Élysées, fireworks and dancing in the streets.

July–August *Fête des Tuileries:* Jardin des Tuileries becomes a traditional fun fair from noon until late at night. www.feteforaine-jardindestuileries.com

Paris, Quartier d'Été: Open-air music, plays and dance in venues around the city. www.quartierdete.com

Festival de Cinéma en Plein Air: Films in the original language screened in Parc de la Villette, nightly at dusk except Monday. www.villette.com

Paris Plages: For four weeks, sand is spread along the banks of the Seine and Bassin de la Villette. Free activities and concerts. www.parisinfo.com

August–September *Festival Classique au Vert:* Classical open-air concerts on weekend afternoons in Parc Floral near Château de Vincennes. www.parcfloraldeparis.com

La Villette Jazz Festival: Two-week jazz festival in Parc de la Villette and nearby venues, including children's jazz concerts. www.jazzalavillette.com

October *Nuit Blanche:* One-night festival of contemporary arts, running all night in churches, theatres, galleries and train stations. www.paris.fr

November *Paris Photo:* Aiming to be the world's best photography event, this week-long exhibition is held at Carrousel du Louvre. www.parisphoto.fr

December *Paris Illumine Paris:* Christmas lights, especially along the Champs-Élysées, and store window displays in boulevard Haussmann.

Open-air ice rinks: At Hôtel de Ville, Montparnasse and other venues.

ÎLE-DE-FRANCE

March–April *Banlieues Bleues:* A month of jazz and blues concerts throughout the Seine-Saint-Denis area. www.banlieuesbleues.org

June *Médiévales:* Medieval pageant and tournament in Provins. www.provins-medieval.com

Le Mois Molière: Theatre, music and street entertainment honouring the great playwright around Versailles. www.moismoliere.com

June–July *Festival de Saint-Denis Basilique:* Classical music at the Basilica and nearby venues. www.festival-saint-denis-fr

Festival d'Auvers-sur-Oise: Classical music festival of piano, choral and chamber music in churches and the château. www.festival-auvers.com

July–August *Fête des Loges de Saint-Germain-en-Laye:* A fair held in the former hunting forest. www.saintgermainenlaye.fr

August *Rock en Seine:* Held in Parc Saint-Cloud, this three-day event draws headlining rock bands. www.rockenseine.com

September–October *Festival d'Île-de-France:* Concerts and shows in castles, abbeys and churches throughout the region. www.festival-idf.fr

September–December *Festival d'Automne:* International arts festival of new and often specially commissioned works in music, dance, cinema and art, throughout the Île de France. www.festival-automne.com

Getting there

BY AIR

Roissy Charles de Gaulle Airport

25km (15.5 miles) to city centre

🚈 35 minutes

🚌 45–60 minutes

🚕 30–45 minutes

Orly Airport

15km (9 miles) to city centre

🚈 40 minutes

🚌 30 minutes

🚕 20–30 minutes

Paris has two main airports (tel: 3950 in France, 00 33 170 36 39 50 from abroad; www.aeroportsdeparis.fr): Roissy Charles de Gaulle, where most international flights arrive, and Orly. Numerous carriers operate direct flights from Canada and the US, including American Airlines, Delta and Air Canada. From the UK, British Airways, Flybe and easyJet operate regular services; from Australia, Qantas is the major carrier. France's national airline, Air France (tel: 0820 320 820 in France; 0871 66 33777 in the UK; 800/237-2747 in the US; www.airfrance.com) has scheduled flights from Britain, mainland Europe and beyond, to both main airports. Approximate flying times to Paris: London (1 hour), Dublin (1.5 hours), New York (8 hours), West Coast USA (12 hours), Vancouver (10 hours), Montréal (7.5 hours), Sydney (23 hours), Auckland (21 hours).

Ticket prices tend to be highest from Easter to September. City break packages may offer even more savings if a Saturday night is included. Check with the airlines, travel agents and internet for best deals.

BY RAIL

The Eurostar passenger train service (tel: 08432 186186 in Britain; www.eurostar.com) from London St Pancras via the Channel Tunnel to Paris Gare du Nord takes 2 hours 15 minutes, bringing you into the heart of the city. There are six major railway stations, each handling traffic to different parts of France and Europe – Gare de Lyon, Gare du Nord, Gare de l'Est, Gare St-Lazare, Gare d'Austerlitz and Gare Montparnasse. French Railways (SNCF; www.sncf.com) operates high-speed trains (TGV – *Train à Grande Vitesse*) to Paris from main stations throughout France.

BY SEA
Ferry companies operate regular services from England and Ireland to France, with rail links to Paris. Crossing time: 75 minutes to 6 hours (England); 14–18 hours (Ireland).

BY ROAD
There are several ways to cross the Channel with a car. The fastest way is via the Channel Tunnel between Folkestone and Calais (journey time: 35 minutes; tel: 08705 35 35 35 in the UK, 0810 63 03 04 in France; www.eurotunnel.com). The alternative is a ferry crossing (see www.discoverferries.co.uk for routes); Dover–Calais has many daily crossings (journey time: 90 minutes): SeaFrance (tel: 0871 22 22 500 in the UK, 03 21 17 70 26 in France, www.seafrance.com) and P&O Ferries (tel: 08716 645 645 in the UK, 0825 120156 in France, www.poferries.com). From Calais it's motorway all the way to Paris via the A26 then the A1 which joins the *périphérique* (the ring road which runs right round the city).

Getting around

PUBLIC TRANSPORT
Internal flights Air France is the leading domestic airline – information (tel: 0820 320 820). Daily departures from Orly and Roissy/Charles-de-Gaulle airports connect Paris with major French cities/towns in an average flight time of one hour.

RER The RER (pronounced 'ehr-oo-ehr') is the fast suburban rail service, which also serves the city centre. There are five lines *(lignes):* A, B, C, D and E and the RER is connected with the métro and SNCF suburban network. Services run 4:45am to 1:30am, with trains every 12 minutes.

Métro Paris's underground with more than 300 stations ensures you are never more than 500m (550yds) from a métro stop. Lines are numbered

1 to 14; choose your direction by the name of the station at the end of the line. Follow the orange *correspondance* signs to change lines. The métro runs daily from 5:30am to 12:30–1am (2:15am Fri and Sat). See www.ratp.fr for more information and interactive maps.

Buses Buses are a good way to see Paris (especially route 24 and Balabus sightseeing route). They run from 6:30am to 8:30pm with a reduced service thereafter. About half the routes do not run on Sunday (check at the bus stop). However, there is a good "Noctilien" nightbus service. Bus tickets are the same as those for the métro and you can change routes once within one 90-minute journey on one ticket.

Boat The Batobus river shuttle (tel: 0825 05 01 01; www.batobus.com) every 15 to 25 minutes, has eight stops on either side of the Seine at landmarks between the Eiffel Tower and the Jardin des Plantes (10–9 May–Sep; 10–7 late Mar, Apr, Oct; 10:30–4:30 Nov–early Jan. No service Feb to late Mar).

Taxis There are many taxi stands or you can hail a taxi if its roof light is illuminated. (Changes proposed for December 2011 include a green/red light to show if the taxi is available or not, and automatic receipts.) Fares are metered with surcharges for each piece of luggage, journeys after 5pm and before 10am, and for ordering a taxi by phone (01 45 30 30 30 for all firms, or G7 speaks English: 01 41 27 66 99). If you are elderly, infirm or travelling with small children, you should be ushered to the front of the taxi queue.

DRIVING
- Driving is on the right; seatbelts must be worn at all times.
- Speed limits on toll motorways *(autoroutes)*: 130kph/80mph (110kph/68mph when wet); non-toll motorways and dual carriageways: 110kph/68mph (100kph/62mph when wet); Paris ring road *(périphérique)*: 80kph/50mph; country roads: 90kph/56mph; urban roads: 50kph/31mph.
- Random breath-testing takes place. Never drink alcohol before driving.
- Unleaded petrol is available in 95 *(essence sans plomb)* and 98 *(super sans plomb)* octane. Diesel *(Gasoil* or *Gazole)* and LPG *(GPL)* are also available. Filling stations may consist of little more than kerbside pumps.

- If you break down on a motorway *(autoroute)* use the orange-coloured emergency phones (located every 2km/1.2 miles).
- You must carry with you the vehicle's registration document, your full valid national driving licence and a current insurance certificate, as well as a reflective warning triangle and *gilet* (high-visbility jacket).
- Driving in the city itself is difficult and not recommended.

CAR RENTAL

Car rental companies have desks at Roissy/Charles-de-Gaulle and Orly airports, and in Paris itself. Car rental is expensive, but airlines and tour operators offer fly-drive, and French Railways (SNCF) offers train/car, packages that are cheaper than renting locally.

ARRONDISSEMENTS

Paris is divided into 20 *arrondissements* (districts), which spiral clockwise from the city centre. The central *arrondissements* are numbered 1 to 8:

1 (75001): heart of the Right Bank, the Louvre and the Île de la Cité.

2 (75002): the commercial district around the Opéra.

3 and **4** (75003 and 75004): the Marais district and the Île St-Louis.

5 (75005): the Latin Quarter and the Left Bank.

6 (75006): the St-Germain district.

7 (75007): residential Faubourg St-Germain and the Tour Eiffel.

8 (75008): the chic broad avenues radiating out from the Arc de Triomphe.

FARES AND TICKETS

Buy métro/bus tickets in a *carnet* of 10 tickets (€11.60). A Paris Visite travel card (€9–€49.40; children 4–11 half fare) is valid in and around Paris for 1, 2, 3 or 5 consecutive days on the métro, RER, buses, Montmartre funicular, tramway and SNCF Île-de-France. Available at all stations.

The Paris Museum Pass entitles you to free entry, without queuing, to permanent exhibitions in more than 60 museums and to monuments. A 2-day pass costs €32, a 4-day pass €48 and a 6-day pass €64 from the Paris Tourist Office and at sights.

All young people under 26 from EU countries get free entry to French national museums on production of their ID. Over 60s can get discounts on SNCF trains, but not Parisian public transport. Some museums and attractions will also give discounts to older visitors with ID.

Being there

TOURIST OFFICES

Head Office
Office de Tourisme de Paris (Paris Tourism Bureau), 25 rue des Pyramides, 75001 Paris
 www.parisinfo.com Daily 10–7, Sun and public hols 11–7

Branches in Paris
Anvers (72 boulevard de Rochechouart) Daily 10–6
Gare de Lyon Mon–Sat 8–6
Gare du Nord Daily 8–6
Montmartre (21 place du Tertre) Daily 10–7
Gare de l'Est Mon–Sat 8–7

Porte de Versailles Daily during trade fairs 11–7

Paris Île-de-France
Paris Roissy-CDG airport terminals 2C,2D, 2E, 2F, T1 arrivals Daily
Paris Orly airport: terminal Orly Sud, gate L 7:15am–9:45pm
Versailles: 2bis avenue de Paris Apr–Sep Tue–Sun 9–7, Mon 10–6; Oct–Mar Tue–Sat 10–6, Sun–Mon 11–5
Disneyland® Resort Paris: place François Truffaut Daily 9:20–8:45

MONEY
The French unit of currency is the euro (€). Coins are issued in 1, 2, 5, 10, 20 and 50 cents denominations and €1 and €2. There are 100 cents in €1. Notes (bills) are in €5, €10, €20, €50, €100, €200 and €500 denominations.

You can exchange travellers' cheques at some banks and at bureaux de change, but transactions are subject to a hefty commission. Credit and debit cards are widely accepted, and you can use them with a four-digit PIN to withdraw cash at ATMs – beware commission charges. Some banks offer prepaid cash cards. Filling stations may not accept foreign cards.

TIPS AND GRATUITIES

	Yes ✓ No ✗	
Hotels (service included)	✓	change
Restaurants (service included)	✓	change
Cafés/bars (service included)	✓	change
Taxis	✓	€1.50
Tour guides	✓	€1.50
Porters	✓	€1.50
Toilets	✓	change

POSTAL AND INTERNET SERVICES

Post offices are identified by a yellow "La Poste" sign. The main office at 52 rue du Louvre is open Mon–Sat 7:30am–6am, Sun 10am–6am. The branch at 71 avenue des Champs-Elysées is open Mon–Fri 9–7:30, Sat 10–6:30.

There are many internet cafés in Paris. The Milk chain (www.milklub.com) is open 24 hours at various locations, including Les Halles (31 boulevard Sébastopol) and Saint-Michel (53 rue de la Harpe). Many hotels offer free WiFi and there are WiFi hotspots in some public places.

TELEPHONES

All telephone numbers in France comprise 10 digits. Paris and Île de France numbers all begin with 01. There are no area codes, simply dial the number. Most public phones use a phone-card *(télécarte)* sold in units of 50 or 120 from France Telecom shops, post offices, tobacconists and railway stations. Cheap rates apply Mon–Fri 7pm–8am, Sat–Sun all day.

International dialling codes

UK: 00 44

Ireland: 00 353

USA/Canada: 00 1

Australia: 00 61

Germany: 00 49

Spain: 00 34

Emergency telephone numbers

Police: 17

Fire: 18

Ambulance: 15

Doctor (24-hour call out):

01 47 07 77 77

EMBASSIES AND CONSULATES

UK ☎ 01 44 51 31 00

Germany ☎ 01 53 83 45 00

USA ☎ 01 43 12 22 22

Netherlands ☎ 01 40 62 33 00

Spain ☎ 01 44 43 18 00

HEALTH ADVICE

Sun advice July and August are the sunniest (and hottest) months. When sightseeing cover up or apply a sunscreen and take plenty of fluids.

Drugs Pharmacies – recognized by their green cross sign – have qualified staff who can offer medical advice, provide first aid and prescribe a wide range of drugs, some are available by prescription *(ordonnance)* only.

Safe water It is quite safe to drink tap water in Paris and all over France, but never drink from a tap marked *eau non potable* (not drinking water). Mineral water is fairly cheap and widely available.

PERSONAL SAFETY

Theft of wallets and handbags is fairly common in Paris. Be aware of scruffy children – they may be working the streets in gangs. Report loss or theft to the Police Municipale (blue uniforms). To be safe:

- Watch your bag on the métro, in areas like the Champs-Elysées and Beaubourg and in museum queues.
- Cars should be well-secured.
- Put valuables in your hotel safe.

ELECTRICITY

The power supply in Paris is 220 volts. Sockets accept two-round-pin (or increasingly three-round-pin) plugs, so an adaptor is needed for most non-Continental appliances. A transformer is needed for appliances operating on 110–120 volts (for example, from North America).

OPENING HOURS

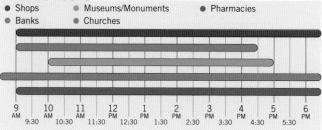

In addition to the times shown above, some shops close noon–2pm and all day Sunday and Monday. Large department stores open 9:30–6:30 and until 9 or 10pm one or two days a week. Some banks have extended hours, including Saturday morning but most close weekends. Museum and monument opening times vary: national museums close Tuesday (except the Trianon Palace, the Musée d'Orsay and Versailles which close Monday); other museums usually close Monday. Note that museum and gallery ticket desks close 30 to 45 minutes before general closing time.

LANGUAGE

You will usually hear well-enunciated French in Paris, spoken quite quickly and in a variety of accents, as many Parisians come from the provinces. English is spoken by those involved in the tourist trade and by many in the centre of Paris. However, attempts to speak French will always be appreciated. Below is a list of some helpful words and phrases.

please	*s'il vous plaît*	how are you?	*comment ça va?*
thank you	*merci*	do you speak	*parlez-vous Anglais?*
hello	*bonjour*	English?	
goodbye	*au revoir*	I don't understand	*je ne comprends pas*
good evening	*bonsoir*	how much?	*combien?*
goodnight	*bonne nuit*	open/closed	*ouvert/fermé*
sorry	*pardon*	today	*aujourd'hui*
excuse me	*excusez moi*	tomorrow	*demain*
hotel room	*la chambre*	one/two night(s)	*une/deux nuit(s)*
single (room)	*une personne*	breakfast	*le petit déjeuner*
double (room)	*deux personnes*	bathroom	*la salle de bain*
per person	*par personne*	toilet	*les toilettes*
bank	*la banque*	banknote	*le billet*
exchange office	*le bureau de change*	travellers' cheque	*le chèque de voyage*
post office	*la poste*	credit card	*la carte de crédit*
coin	*la pièce*	change	*la monnaie*
lunch	*le déjeuner*	bill	*l'addition*
dinner	*le dîner*	drink	*la boisson*
table	*la table*	beer	*la bière*
waiter/waitress	*le garçon/la serveuse*	wine	*le vin*
water	*l'eau*	coffee	*le café*
airport	*l'aéroport*	single/return	*simple/retour*
train	*le train*	car	*la voiture*
bus	*l'autobus*	petrol/gasoline	*l'essence*
station	*la gare*	bus stop	*l'arrêt d'autobus*
ticket	*le billet*	where is...?	*où est...?*

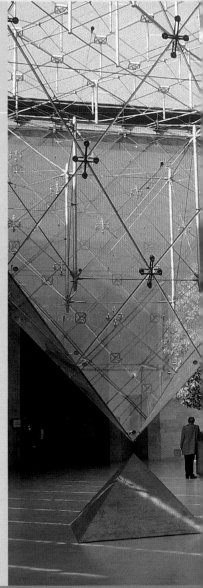

Best places to see

Arc de Triomphe

www.monum.fr

The focus of all France's national celebrations, Napoleon's iconic arch stands on the main axis of the capital and commands a grand vista across the city.

After the battle of Austerlitz in 1806, Napoléon I promised his soldiers, "You will march home through the arches of victory." The 50m-high (164ft) Arc de Triomphe was completed 30 years later when Louis-Philippe I, France's last reigning monarch, dedicated it to the glory of the armies of the Republic and the Empire. It was later dedicated to the memory of an unknown soldier of the Republic who died during World War I. "O vast pile cut out by history! A heap of stones atop a heap of glory!" wrote Victor Hugo, and indeed, the pillars of the arch bear the names of hundreds of France's heroes and the battles in which they fought.

For more than 150 years, it marked the final point of a city perspective stretching from the Arc de Triomphe du Carrousel near the Louvre, through the place de la Concorde, and along the Champs-Élysées, until in 1989 the huge Grande Arche de la Défense lined up behind it as the centrepiece of a new commerical sector of Paris.

Climb the 284 steps to the mezzanine (the stairs are narrow and queues can be long) and you will find an exhibition called "Between War and Peace" that explains the

arch's history and construction. Interactive videos enable you to examine the monument's fine detail and the bas-reliefs around the pediment including Cortot's *Triumph of Napoleon* and the departure of the Marseillese volunteers of 1792 who gave their name to France's national anthem. There is also a camera showing the people passing the the tomb of the unknown soldier below. His ashes were buried here in 1921 and each evening since 1923 the eternal flame has been reignited at 6:30pm.

Climb a few more stairs and you emerge on the very top for a splendid view of the city and especially the 12 avenues radiating out from the monument which give the area the name l'Étoile (the star).

✚ 6H ✉ Place Charles de Gaulle, 75008 ☎ 01 55 37 73 77 🕐 Apr–Sep daily 10am–11pm; Oct–Mar 10–10. Closed 1 Jan, 1 May, morning of 8 May, morning of 14 Jul, morning of 11 Nov, 25 Dec ✋ Moderate 🚇 Charles de Gaulle-Étoile 🚌 22, 30, 31, 52, 73, 92 ❓ Shop and toilets in mezzanine

2 # Centre Georges Pompidou

www.centrepompidou.fr

This spacious and convivial art centre, in the heart of historic Paris, houses under one roof all forms of modern and contemporary art.

With 6 million visitors a year, the Centre Georges Pompidou is now one of Paris's top sights. Yet at the time it was built, close to the historic Marais which is famous for its elegant architecture, the "refinery", as Rogers and Piano's post-modern building was nicknamed, deeply shocked French people. In fact, the revolutionary concept of this open-plan "house

of culture for all" ensured its success and brought life back to the district.

The centre's main asset, the Musée National d'Art Moderne, reached by the external escalator, gained extra exhibition space in the process and a new chronological presentation of its collection. The museum is dedicated to the main trends of art from 1905 to the present day. Modern art is displayed on level 5. Particularly well represented are Fauvism (Dufy, Derain, Matisse), Cubism (Braque, Picasso, Léger), Dadaism, Surrealism (Dalí, Miró), Expressionism (Soutine, Kirchner, Modigliani and to a lesser extent Chagall), various forms of abstract art (Kandinsky, Klee, but also Poliakoff, Dubuffet and the CoBrA movement), and pre-1960 American painting. Level 4 is devoted to contemporary art. Drawing on the centre's collection of some 60,000 works, exponents of New Realism, Pop Art and Minimalist art are included. Special exhibitions are on level 6.

The centre also houses a library, the Institute for Acoustic and Musical Research, an exhibition hall, a cinema, a reconstruction of Brancusi's workshop and a children's workshop.

➕ 16M ✉ Place Georges-Pompidou, 75004 ☎ 01 44 78 12 33 🕐 Centre: Wed–Mon. Modern art museum and exhibitions: 11–9. Library: weekdays 12–10; weekends 11–10. Brancusi workshop 2–6 👋 Free access; museum: expensive (includes Brancusi workshop, children's workshop, exhibitions and level 6) 🍴 Restaurant (€€), café and snack bar 🚇 Rambuteau, Hôtel de Ville, Châtelet 🚌 21, 29, 38, 47, 58, 69, 70, 72, 74, 75, 76, 81, 85, 96 ❓ Audioguides, ATM, shops, post office

3 Les Champs-Élysées

www.monum.fr

For most visitors this prestigious avenue epitomizes French elegance, but it is also a dazzling place of entertainment and a luxury shopping mall.

In the late 17th century, André Le Nôtre designed a gently rising alleyway as an extension of the Jardin des Tuileries. This later lost its rustic appearance and became a fashionable avenue lined with elegant restaurants and cafés. Nowadays it is the traditional venue for a variety of events such as the Paris Marathon, the arrival of the Tour de France and the march past on 14 July, which celebrates France's national day. But "les Champs" (the fields) is also a place where people of all ages can come to just relax and feel alive.

The lower section, stretching from the place de la Concorde (with breathtaking views along the whole length of the avenue) to the Rond-Point des Champs-Élysées, is laid out as an English-style park shaded by imposing chestnut trees. On the left of the avenue are the Grand Palais and Petit Palais, two temples of the arts, while on the right is a monument to the French Resistance hero, Jean Moulin, who was reburied in the Panthéon on 19 December 1964.

The upper section stretches from the Rond-Point, designed by Le Nôtre, to the Arc de Triomphe. This is the "modern" part of the avenue, with its pavements

now revamped and restored to their former comfortable width. Banks, cinemas, airline offices, car showrooms and large cafés spread out onto the pavements, lining the way to the place de l'Étoile. Fashion boutiques cluster along the arcades running between the Champs-Élysées and the parallel rue de Ponthieu. Some shops remain open well into the night and the bustle only quietens down in the early hours of the morning.

✚ 9K ✉ Avenue des Champs-Élysées, 75008 🍴 Choice of restaurants (€–€€€) 🚇 Concorde, Champs-Élysées Clemenceau, Franklin D. Roosevelt, George V, Charles de Gaulle-Étoile 🚌 42, 73

4 Les Invalides

www.invalides.org

This is one of Paris's most imposing architectural ensembles, built around two churches and housing several museums.

The Hôtel National des Invalides was commissioned by Louis XIV as a home for wounded soldiers. It is a splendid example of 17th-century architecture, the classical austerity of its 200m-long (656ft) facade being offset by the baroque features of the Église du Dôme, with its gilt dome glittering above the slate roofs of the stone buildings. The huge esplanade filling the gap between the river and the monumental entrance enhances the majesty of the building.

Entry to the museums is from the arcaded main courtyard. The Musée de l'Armée has one of the richest collections of its kind in the world. On display are antique arms and armour from the 13th to the 17th centuries, an exhibition on world wars and 600 classic French cannons. You do not have to be a fan of French military history to find the department covering the period from Louis XIV to Napoléon I interesting. Using boots and breastplates as much as swords and guns to tell the story, it covers a time of many wars and details France's part in the American War of Independence.

On the other side of the courtyard, the halls devoted to General Charles de Gaulle use archive film and multimedia to tell the life of France's greatest statesman of the 20th century.

On the far side of the courtyard is the entrance to St-Louis-des-Invalides, the soldiers' church, which contains a colourful collection of flags brought back from various campaigns.

The Église du Dôme, built for royal use by Jules Hardouin-Mansart, is a striking contrast: an elegant facade with two tiers of Doric and Corinthian columns and an imposing gilt dome surmounted by a slender lantern. The splendid interior decoration is enhanced by the marble floor. The open circular crypt houses Napoleon's red porphyry tomb.

➕ 18P 📧 129 rue de Grenelle, 75007 ☎ 08 10 11 33 99
🕐 Apr–Sep daily 10–6; Oct–Mar 10–5. Closed Oct–Jun
1st Mon of month, 1 Jan, 1 May, 1 Nov, 25 Dec
💷 Moderate 🍴 Restaurant (€) 🚇 Invalides, La Tour
Maubourg, Varenne 🚌 28, 49, 63, 69, 82, 83, 87, 92
❓ Audiovisual shows, guided tours, shops

5 Le Louvre

www.louvre.fr

This former royal palace, which celebrated its bicentenary in 1993, is today one of the largest museums in the world.

THE PALACE

Excavations in 1977 under the Cour Carrée, the courtyard surrounded by the oldest part of the palace, led to the discovery of the original castle built around 1200 by King Philippe-Auguste. The tour of the foundations of this medieval Louvre, including the the keep, the moat and the outer wall, starts from the entrance hall under the glass pyramid.

The first 16th-century palace, built by Pierre Lescot in the style of the Italian Renaissance, was enlarged round the Cour Carrée and along the Seine during the following 200 years. Louis XIV enclosed the Cour Carrée with the stately colonnade that faces the Church of St-Germain-l'Auxerrois. Soon afterwards, however, the king left for Versailles and the palace was neglected by the royal family and the court.

Building was resumed by Napoleon, who built part of the north wing and erected the exquisite Arc de Triomphe du Carrousel. During the second half of the 19th century, Napoleon III completed the Louvre along its rue de Rivoli side.

THE MUSEUM

The collections are divided into eight departments:
● Egyptian Antiquities include the pink granite *Great Sphinx of Tanis*, a huge *head of Amenophis IV-Akhenaten* and the famous *Seated Scribe*.

- The most remarkable exhibits in the Near Eastern Antiquities department must be the *Assyrian winged bulls*.
- The Greek, Etruscan and Roman Antiquities department contains many masterpieces: don't miss the *Vénus de Milo*, *Winged Victory of Samothrace* and Greco-Roman sculpture in the Salle des Cariatides.
- The painting collections comprise a fine selection from the Italian school (Fra Angelico, Leonardo da Vinci, Giotto, Veronese, Titian, Raphael), the French school (Poussin, Watteau, Georges de la Tour), the Dutch school (Rembrandt, Rubens, Vermeer) and Spanish masters (Murillo, Goya and El Greco).
- French sculpture is well represented and includes works by Goujon, Houdon and Pradier.
- In the Richelieu wing are beautiful tapestries and historic items such as Charlemagne's sword.
- The department of Prints and Drawings displays its fragile works on paper in temporary exhibitions.
- A new Islamic art gallery opened in the Cour Visconti in 2010 to display some 2,000 objects from three continents and 13 centuries.

➕ 13M ✉ 99 rue de Rivoli, 75001. Main entrance via Pyramid ☎ Switchboard: 01 40 20 50 50; reception desk: 01 40 20 53 17; visitors with disabilities: 01 40 20 59 90 🕐 Wed–Mon 9–6 (until 10pm Wed and Fri). Closed 1 Jan, 1 May, 11 Nov, 25 Dec ♿ Moderate, reduced fee after 6 Wed and Fri, free 1st Sun of month. To avoid a long wait, buy your ticket in advance online 🍽 Restaurants (€ and €€) and cafés below Pyramid and in Carrousel du Louvre 🚇 Palais-Royal/Musée du Louvre 🚌 21, 24, 27, 39, 48, 68, 69, 72, 81, 95 ❓ Guided tours, lectures, concerts, film shows, shops

6 Musée d'Orsay

www.musee-orsay.fr

Once a mainline railway station, the Musée d'Orsay has been successfully converted into one of Paris's three major art museums.

Built in 1900, the Gare d'Orsay was narrowly saved from demolition by a daring plan to turn it into a museum dedicated to all forms of art from 1848 to 1914, and intended as the chronological link between the Louvre and the Musée National d'Art Moderne. The Musée d'Orsay was inaugurated by President Mitterrand in 1986.

In 2009, the museum embarked on an extensive renovation programme, scheduled to end in March 2011, although the museum itself remained open throughout. The museum's website is updated each night to show which works are on display.

The aim of the reorganization was to give a visit coherence, and improve the context – the colour of the walls and the lighting – in which the works are seen. Thus Impressionists, including Manet, Degas, Monet, Cézanne, Renoir and Sisley, are together on the fifth floor under the glass canopy. Van Gogh,

Gauguin, the school of Pont-Aven, Seurat, the Douanier Rousseau and other post-Impressionists occupy the middle level on the side of the rue de Lille, while the Pavillon Amont will be home to the Nabi school – the post-Impressionist avant garde of the 1890s who included Bonnard and Vuillard. Here you will also find decorative arts, of foreign schools as well as by masters of art nouveau such as Lalique and Guimard. Temporary exhibitions are held in the Salle des Colonnes.

One constant is that the original station clock will continue to oversee the whole display. Another is the masterpieces that draw the crowds. Here you will find works by Ingrès, Delacroix, Corot and Courbet, as well as Manet's *Olympia* and his *Déjuner sur l'herbe*, *Blue Dancers* by Degas, Monet's *Houses of Parliament* and *Rouen Cathedral*, Cézanne's *Card Players*, Renoir's *Bal du moulin de la Galette*, Van Gogh's *Bedroom at Arles*.

🚇 12M ✉ 1 rue de la Légion d'Honneur, 75007 ☎ 01 40 49 48 14 🕐 Tue–Sun 9:30–6; late night: Thu 9:45. Closed Mon, 1 Jan, 1 May, 25 Dec ✋ Moderate, free 1st Sun of month; to avoid long queues buy tickets in advance online 🍴 Restaurant (€), café (€) 🚇 Solférino; RER Musée d'Orsay 🚌 24, 63, 68, 69, 73, 83, 84, 94 ⛴ Batobus ❓ Audioguides, guided tours, shops, concerts, film shows

7 Notre-Dame

www.cathedraledeparis.com

This masterpiece of Gothic architecture is one of Paris's most famous landmarks and one of France's most visited religious monuments.

In 1163, the Bishop of Paris, Maurice de Sully, ordered the building of the cathedral, which took nearly 200 years to complete. One of the architects involved was Pierre de Montreuil, who also built the nearby Sainte-Chapelle (➤ 93). Some of its statues were mutilated during the Revolution and the cathedral also lost its original bells, except the *"gros bourdon"*, known as Emmanuel, which is traditionally heard on occasions of national importance. The richly decorated portals are surmounted by statues of kings of Judaea, restored by Viollet-le-Duc in the 19th century. Above the central rose window, a colonnade links the elegant twin towers; there is a grand view from the south tower, if you can face the 387-step climb.

The nave is 130m (426ft) long, 48m (157ft) wide and 35m (115ft) high; the side chapels are richly decorated with paintings, sculptures and funeral monuments. The former vestry, on the right of the chancel, houses the Cathedral Treasure, which includes a piece of the Holy Cross.

Under the Parvis de Notre Dame, from which all distances to Paris within France are measured, lies the archaeological crypt holding remnants from the Roman occupation of Gaul to the early 19th century. Here you can see the original ramparts and relics of the Roman town.

🕂 25Q ✉ Cathedral: place du Parvis de Notre-Dame, 75004. Tower: rue du Cloître Notre-Dame to left of cathedral. Archaeological crypt: in square near police headquarters ☎ Cathedral: 01 42 34 56 10. Tower: 01 53 10 07 00. Archaeological crypt: 01 55 42 50 10 🕓 Cathedral: Mon–Fri 8–6:45, Sat–Sun 8–7:15; closed some religious feast days. Treasure: Mon–Fri 9:30–6, Sat 9:30–6:30, Sun 1:30–6:30. Tower: Apr–Sep daily 10–6:30 (Jul–Aug Sat–Sun 10am–11pm); Oct–Mar daily 10–5:30. Archaeological crypt: Tue–Sun 10–6 💰 Cathedral: free. Treasure: inexpensive. Towers: moderate. Archaeological crypt: inexpensive 🍴 Left Bank (€–€€) 🚇 Cité, Saint-Michel 🚌 21, 24, 27, 38, 47, 85, 96 ❓ Guided tours (free, times vary), audioguide (moderate)

8 Les Quais

Walk along the banks of the Seine between the pont de la Concorde and the pont de Sully for some of Paris's finest views.

In 1992, the river banks from the pont d'Iéna, where the Tour Eiffel stands, to the pont de Sully, at the tip of the Île St-Louis, were added to UNESCO's list of World Heritage Sites. Here the townscape has an indefinable charm inspired by the harmonious blend of colours: the pale greys and blues of the water and the sky, the soft green of the trees lining the embankment and the mellow stone colour of the historic buildings. Parisians have been strolling along the embankments for centuries, window-shopping, browsing through the *bouquinistes'* stalls or simply watching the activity on both sides of the river.

THE RIGHT BANK

Start from the pont du Carrousel and walk upriver past the imposing facade of the Louvre. From pont Neuf, enjoy a marvellous view of the Conciergerie on the Île de la Cité, or admire the birds and exotic fish on the quai de la Mégisserie. Continue past the Hôtel de Ville towards the lovely pont Marie leading to the peaceful Île St-Louis. Cross over to the Left Bank.

THE LEFT BANK

The familiar green boxes that form the stalls of the *bouquinistes* are here as well! Admire the stunning views of Notre-Dame and its magnificent flying buttresses. The quai Saint-Michel is a favourite haunt of students looking for second-hand books. Farther on, stand on the steel, pedestrian, pont des Arts for a romantic view upriver of the historic heart of Paris before walking past the stately facade of the Musée d'Orsay towards the 18th-century pont de la Concorde.

✚ 24Q ✉ Quai du Louvre, quai de la Mégisserie (75001), quai de Gesvres, quai de l'Hôtel de Ville, quai des Célestins (75004), quai de la Tournelle, quai de Montebello, quai St-Michel (75005), quai des Grands Augustins, quai de Conti, quai Malaquais (75006), quai Voltaire, quai Anatole-France (75007) 🍽 Restaurants and cafés along the way, particularly near place du Châtelet and place de l'Hôtel de Ville on the Right Bank, and around place St-Michel on the Left Bank (€–€€€) 🚇 Pont-Neuf, Châtelet, Hôtel de Ville, Pont Marie, St-Michel, Solférino 🚌 24 follows the Left Bank ❓ Boat trips along the Seine from pont de l'Alma right round the islands

9 Sacre-Cœur

www.sacre-coeur-montmartre.com

The white domes and campaniles of this basilica stand out against the skyline, high above the rooftops of the city, on the summit of Montmartre.

The construction of this Roman-Byzantine basilica, designed by Paul Abadie, was a mark of national reconciliation and hope after the bitter defeat suffered by France in the 1870 war against Prussia. Not everyone was reconciled – one of the last redoubts was the Montmartre commune, crushed in 1871, and to this day many Parisians resent the building as an imposition and a symbol of state power. Funds were raised by public subscription (donors' names are inscribed on the interior walls) and work started in 1875, but the basilica took nearly 45 years to build and was not inaugurated until 1919, after another war.

Today the basilica stands 83m (272ft) high on top of Montmartre so those who ascend the dome reach the second-highest point in Paris, and are rewarded with a panoramic view that stretches for 50km (31 miles) around the city. Many visitors, who may have already climbed the many steep steps that lead up to Sacré-Cœur, content

themselves with the breathtaking view over the whole of Paris from the terrace in front of the basilica.

Equally, the basilica's gleaming white travertine domes and belltowers, inside one of which hangs the 19-tonne Savoyarde bell, are visible from all over the city. The interior is richly decorated with golden mosaics that glitter by the light of the many candles lit by pilgrims who come to worship in silence. The original stained-glass windows were destroyed in World War II, but restored soon after. Outside on the right-hand side of the building you will find the entrance to the crypt, which contains a relic said to be the Sacred Heart (Sacré-Cœur) of Christ himself.

✚ 3C ✉ Place du Parvis du Sacré-Cœur, 75018 ☎ 01 53 41 89 00 ⚙ Basilica: daily 6am–10:30pm; dome and crypt: 9–6 (until 7 in summer) ✋ Basilica free; dome and crypt: inexpensive 🅰 Abbesses, Funicular 🚌 Montmartrobus, 30, 54, 85 ❓ Shops; photographs not allowed inside the basilica

10 La Tour Eiffel

www.tour-eiffel.fr

Paris's most famous landmark has been towering above the city for more than 120 years, yet its universal appeal remains constant.

The Tour Eiffel was built by the engineer Gustave Eiffel as a temporary attraction for the 1889 World Exhibition. At the time, its 300m (984ft) height made it the tallest building in the world and an unprecedented technological achievement. It met with instant success, was celebrated by poets and artists, and its spindly silhouette was soon famous all over the world. In spite of this, it was nearly pulled down when the concession expired in 1909 but was saved because of its invaluable radio aerial, joined in 1957 by television aerials. It was later raised by another 20m (66ft) to accommodate a meteorological station. The iron frame weighs 7,300 tonnes, yet the pressure it exerts on the ground is only 4kg per sq cm; 60 tonnes of paint are used to repaint it every seven years. To celebrate its one hundredth birthday, it was renovated and halogen lighting was installed making it even more spectacular at night.

There are stairs to the first and second levels, and all three levels are accessible by lift. On the first floor (57m/187ft above ground) information about the tower is available; there are also a restaurant, a gift shop and a post office, where letters are postmarked Paris Tour Eiffel.

The second floor (115m/377ft above ground) offers fine views of Paris, several boutiques and a restaurant appropriately named Jules Verne.

For a spectacular aerial view of the capital go up to the third floor (276m/905ft above ground). There is also a reconstruction of Gustave Eiffel's study and panoramic viewing tables showing 360-degree photos of Paris with the city's landmarks.

✚ 6M ✉ Champ de Mars, 75007 ☎ 08 92 70 12 39
🕐 Jan to mid-Jun, Sep–Dec daily 9:30am–11:45pm,
(stairs until 6); mid-Jun to Aug daily 9am–12:45am 🖑 Lift
(elevator): 1st–2nd floors inexpensive–moderate, 3rd floor
expensive 🍴 Restaurants (€–€€€) 🚇 Bir-Hakeim;
RER Champ de Mars 🚌 42, 69, 72, 82, 87

Best things to do

Great cafés

Angelina

The fashion world has long gathered in this elegant belle époque tearoom near the Tuileries, founded by an Austrian pastry chef.

✉ 226 rue de Rivoli, 75001 ☎ 01 42 60 82 00 Ⓜ Tuileries

Café de Flore

Cosmopolitan Café de Flore, famous as a haunt for bohemian existentialists – notably writer-philosophers Camus, Simone de Beauvoir and Sartre – is now a hugely popular tourist attraction.

✉ 172 boulevard St-Germain, 75006 ☎ 01 45 48 55 26
Ⓜ St-Germain-des-Prés

Café Martini

This old Italian-style café, just off place des Vosges, stays open until late.

✉ 11 rue du Pas de la Mule, 75004 ☎ 01 42 77 05 04 Ⓜ Chemin Vert, Bastille

Le Café Noir

A younger rock'n'roll crowd is drawn to this buzzy, cool venue, busy day and night.

✉ 36 rue Montmartre, 75002 ☎ 01 40 39 07 36 Ⓜ Sentier

Café de la Paix

This historic café patronized by Oscar Wilde has retained its sumptuous ceiling by Garnier who designed the magnificent Opera House opposite.

✉ Place de l'Opéra ☎ 01 40 07 36 36 Ⓜ Opéra

Chez Prune

Beside fashionable Canal Saint-Martin stands this young, arty place. You'll feel at home if you wear a beret here.

✉ 36 rue Beaurepaire, 75010 ☎ 01 42 41 30 47 Ⓜ République, Jacque Bonsergent

La Closerie des Lilas

Enjoy a drink in this intimate café where poets Baudelaire and Apollinaire and American writer Hemingway once sat. It's a pleasant place for an early evening drink on the sunny terrace.

✉ 171 boulevard du Montparnasse, 75006 ☎ 01 40 51 34 50 Ⓜ Vavin, Port Royal

Les Deux Magots

Les Deux Magots was made famous in the early 20th century by Picasso, the poet André Breton and Parisian intellectuals.

✉ 6 place St-Germain-des-Prés, 75006 ☎ 01 45 48 55 25
Ⓜ St-Germain-des-Prés

Fouquet's

This chic café on the Champs-Elysées is the place to spot French celebrities. Coffee here comes at a price.

✉ 99 Champs-Elysées, 75008 ☎ 01 40 69 60 50 Ⓜ George V

Le Select

American writers and artists have mingled with their Parisian counterparts here since the 1920s.

✉ 99 boulevard du Montparnasse, 75006 ☎ 01 45 48 38 24 Ⓜ Vavin

Best bars

Au Rendez-vous des Amis
Make for this bar on the Butte Montmartre to hear the latest French pop music and mingle with a young, lively crowd.
✉ 23 rue Gabrielle, 75018 ☎ 01 46 06 01 60; www.rdvdesamis.com 🚇 Abbesses, Pigalle
🚌 Montmartrobus

Le Bar Dix
In this poster-hung, studenty cellar bar, a jug of sangria is the thing to order.
✉ 10 rue de l'Odéon, 75006 ☎ 01 43 26 66 83; www.le10bar.com 🚇 Odéon 🚌 58, 63, 86, 87

Bar Hemingway
This bar is preserved in the era when the great author used to drink here in the classy Ritz Hotel. Excellent single malts and cocktails are served.
✉ Ritz Paris, 15 Place Vendôme, 75001 ☎ 01 43 33 65; www.ritzparis.com 🚇 Tuileries, Opéra 🚌 42, 52, 72

Bar Ourcq
In the increasingly fashionable Bassin de la Villette, the canalside setting makes the Bar Ourcq a hip summer hangout.
✉ 68 Quai de la Loire, 75019 ☎ 01 42 40 12 26; www.barourcq.fr 🚇 Laumière, Riquet 🚌 60

Buddha Bar
The smart mezzanine bar puts you eye to eye with the giant buddha, while DJs spin music to help the relaxed atmosphere.
✉ 8–12 rue Boissy d'Anglas, 75008 ☎ 01 53 05 90 00; www.buddhabar.com 🚇 Concorde 🚌 24, 42, 52, 72, 73, 84, 94

Café Charbon

The bar that set off the Oberkampf nightlife boom
is still popular.

✉ 109 rue Oberkampf, 75011 ☎ 01 43 57 57 40;
www.nouveaucasino.net 🚇 Parmentier, Ménilmontant
🚌 96, N12, N23

Costes Bar

Luxurious, romantic, boudouir-themed bar that
attracts the most fashionable crowd in Paris.

✉ Hôtel Costes, 239 rue Saint-Honoré, 75001 ☎ 01 42 44
50 25; www.hotelcostes.com 🚇 Concorde, Madeleine
🚌 72

Le Fumoir

Facing the Louvre, this elegant cocktail bar has its
own library.

✉ 6 rue de l'Amiral Coligny, 75001 ☎ 01 42 92 00 24;
www.lefumoir.com 🚇 Louvre-Rivoli 🚌 21, 67, 69, 72, 74,
76, 81, 85, Balabus

Le Sancerre

A typical Montmartre café-bar with rock music, Le
Sancerre appeals to a young and trendy crowd.

✉ 35 rue des Abbesses, 75018 ☎ 01 42 58 08 20
🚇 Abbesses 🚌 Montmartobus

Le Verre Volé

"The stolen glass" is a tiny bar and wine shop
where you can taste French wine by the glass – or
the bottle.

✉ 67 rue de Lancy, 75010 ☎ 01 48 03 17 34;
www.leverrevole.fr 🚇 République, Jacques Bonsergent
🚌 56, 65, 75

Excellent restaurants

Beauvilliers (€€–€€€)
Gourmet cuisine served in an elegant Napoleon III setting.
✉ 52 rue Lamarck, 75018 ☎ 01 42 55 05 42 🕐 Lunch, dinner; closed Mon lunch, Sun 🚇 Lamarck Caulaincourt

Brasserie Lipp (€€)
Founded in 1880, this restaurant has long been popular with political and literary figures.
✉ 151 boulevard St-Germain, 75006 ☎ 01 45 48 53 91; www.groupe-bertrand.com/lipp 🕐 Daily 9am–1am 🚇 St-Germain-des-Prés

La Coupole (€€)
Famous brasserie from the 1920s with its art deco setting and excellent seafood. Reasonable late-night menu (after 11pm).
✉ 102 boulevard du Montparnasse, 75014 ☎ 01 43 20 14 20; www.flobrasseries.com/coupoleparis 🕐 Daily 8:30am–1am 🚇 Vavin

Le Divellec (€€€)
One of the top seafood restaurants in Paris complete with nautical décor, and very good service.
✉ 107 rue de l'Université, 75007 ☎ 01 45 51 91 96; www.le-divellec.com 🕐 Lunch, dinner; closed Sat, Sun and Christmas 🚇 Invalides

Grand Véfour (€€€)

Haute cuisine with a beautiful view of the Jardin du Palais-Royal.

✉ 17 rue de Beaujolais, 75001 ☎ 01 42 96 56 27; www.grand-vefour.com
🕐 Lunch, dinner; closed Fri night, Sat, Sun and Aug 🚇 Palais-Royal

Guy Savoy (€€€)

A true culinary experience, with delicacies such as poached pigeon and giblets in a beetroot and mushroom millefeuille.

✉ 18 rue Troyon, 75017 ☎ 01 43 80 40 61 🕐 Lunch, dinner; closed Sat lunch, Sun 🚇 Charles de Gaulle-Étoile

Jacques Cagna (€€€)

High-class traditional French cuisine in a 17th-century residence with wood panelling and beams; Dutch paintings to match.

✉ 14 rue des Grands-Augustins, 75006 ☎ 01 43 26 49 39;
www.jacquescagna.com 🕐 Lunch, dinner; closed Sat, Mon lunch, Sun
🚇 Saint-Michel

Pierre Gagnaire (€€€)

One of the most inventive cuisines in Paris. A fascinating, if expensive, adventure in the art of good food.

✉ 6 rue Balzac, 75008 ☎ 01 58 36 12 50; www.pierre-gagnaire.com
🕐 Lunch, dinner; closed Sat, Sun lunch 🚇 George V

Timgad (€€)

Spectacular Moorish interior, innovative, exciting food and attentive service at one of France's best-known Arab restaurants.

✉ 21 rue Brunel, 75017 ☎ 01 45 74 23 70 🕐 Daily 🚇 Argentine

La Tour d'Argent (€€€)

Haute cuisine in exceptional surroundings with remarkable view of Notre-Dame and the river; speciality is *canard* (duck) Tour d'Argent.

✉ 15–17 quai de la Tournelle, 75005 ☎ 01 43 54 23 31;
www.latourdargent.com 🕐 Lunch, dinner; closed Sun, Mon 🚇 Pont Marie

Stunning views

Palais de Chaillot (➤ 126)

Sacré-Coeur (➤ 52–53)

La Tour Eiffel (➤ 54–55)

Tour Montparnasse (➤ 106–107)

Towers of Notre-Dame (➤ 48–49)

Places to take the children

Aquarium de Paris Cinéaqua

See the 43 tanks teeming with 10,000 fish including 25 sharks, then feel some of them in a touch pool.

✉ 5 avenue Albert De Mun, 75016 ☎ 01 40 69 23 23, www.cineaqua.com
🕐 Apr–Sep daily 10–7; Oct–Mar 10–6 🍴 Ozu Japanese restaurant (€)
🚇 Trocadéro, Iéna 🚌 22, 30, 32, 63, 72, 82 ⛴ Batobus

Cirque d'Hiver Bouglione

This annual winter-long event where the flying trapeze was invented is the most famous of several circuses in Paris.

✉ 110 rue Amelot, 75011 ☎ 01 47 00 28 81; www.cirquedhiver.com
🕐 Late Oct–late Feb days vary 💰 Inexpensive 🚇 Filles du Calvaire, Oberkampf, République 🚌 20, 65, 96

Cité des Sciences et de l'Industrie

This cathedral-sized science and technology museum in La Villette includes Cité des Enfants, for the 3 to 5 and 5 to 12 age groups.

✉ 30 avenue Corentin-Cariou, 75019 ☎ 01 40 05 80 00; www.cite-sciences.fr 🕐 Tue–Sat 10–6, Sun 10–7 🚇 Porte de la Villette

Les Guignols de Champs-Élysées

One of the many inexpensive traditional puppet theatres *(guignols)* you will find in squares and parks all over Paris.

✉ Rond-Point des Champs-Élysées/angle des avenues Matignon et Gabriel, 75008 ☎ 01 42 45 38 30, www.theatreguignol.fr 🕐 Wed, Sat, Sun, public hols and school hols at 3, 4 and 5 🚇 Champs-Élysées-Clemenceau, Franklin D. Roosevelt 🚌 28, 32, 52, 80, 83, 93

Jardin d'Acclimatation

For more than 150 years this has been an adventure park, with a host of rides and children's activities.

✉ Bois de Boulogne, 75016 ☎ 01 40 67 90 82; www.jardindacclimatation.fr
🕐 May–Sep daily 10–7, Oct–Apr 10–6 🍴 Various restaurants and cafés
🚇 Sablons, Porte Maillot 🚌 43, 73, 82 🚉 From Porte Maillot every 15–20 min

Jardin des Enfants aux Halles

This adventure playground for 7- to 11-year-olds is closed to adults.
✉ 105 rue Rambuteau, 75001 ☎ 01 45 08 07 18 ; www.paris.fr ⏰ Tue, Thu,
Fri 9–12, 2–6 (4 in winter), Wed, Sat and school hols 10–6 (4 in winter), Sun
and public hols 1–6 (4 in winter) 🚇 Les Halles 🚌 74, 85 ❓ Playleaders in
charge, each child's session limited to one hour

Jardin du Luxembourg

Like most Paris parks, this has plenty for children to do, including
pony rides, model boats to sail and playgrounds.
✉ Enter from boulevard St-Michel, rue de Vaugirard or rue de Médicis
☎ 01 42 64 33 99 ⏰ Daily 7:15–8:15 to dusk depending on the season
🍴 Refreshment kiosks 🚇 Odéon 🚌 21, 27, 38, 58, 82, 83, 84, 85, 89

Jardin des Plantes

The Grande Galerie de l'Évolution offers a spectacular parade of
exhibits, while living creatures animate the menagerie.
Grande Galerie de l'Évolution: ✉ 36 rue Geoffroy Saint-Hilaire, 75010 ☎ 01
40 79 54 79; www.mnhn.fr ⏰ Wed–Mon 10–6. Ménagerie: ✉ 57 rue Cuvier,
75005 ☎ 01 40 79 37 94; www.mnhn.fr ⏰ Summer daily 9–6; winter 9–5
🚇 Jussieu, Gare d'Austerlitz 🚌 24, 57, 61, 63, 67, 89, 91 🚢 Batobus

Musée Grévin

Wax figures of the famous, from Henry VIII to Barack Obama.
✉ 10 boulevard Montmartre, 75009 ☎ 01 47 70 85 05; www.grevin.com
⏰ Mon–Fri 10–6:30; Sat–Sun 10–7 🚇 Grands Boulevards 🚌 20, 39, 48, 67,
74, 85

Visite des Égouts de Paris

For the family that wants to do something different – an hour-long
trip through the sewers of Paris.
✉ Pont de l'Alma, rive gauche (Left Bank), opposite 93 quai d'Orsay, 75007
☎ 01 53 68 27 81; www.paris.fr ⏰ May–Sep Sat–Wed 11–5; Oct–Apr 11–4
🚇 Alma-Marceau 🚌 63, 80

Activities

Walking: under the *Paris respire* ("Paris breathes") scheme, motorized traffic is banned on Sundays along the banks of the Seine and the Canal Saint-Martin and many other parts of the city. Paris respire: ☎ www.deplacements.paris.fr 🕓 Sun, times vary but mostly 9–5. Paris Walks: ☎ 01 48 09 21 40; www.paris-walks.com 🕓 Daily 10:30 and 2:30, different walks every day ✋ Expensive

Cycling: the Vélib system of short-term bike rental is a huge success. Download the guide from the website or follow the instructions on the bike rack and sign up for a day or a week. ✉ Bike racks every 300m (330 yards) around the city, return the bike to any rack ☎ 01 30 79 79 30; www.velib.paris.fr ✋ Inexpensive (first 30 min free)

Take to the water: as well as the Batobus tourist shuttle, you can take a cruise with commentary, or take a two-hour boat trip along the tree-shaded Canal Saint-Martin. Batobus: ✉ 8 piers between Tour Eiffel and Jardin des Plantes ☎ 08 25 05 01 01; www.batobus.com 🕓 Daily every 15–30 min, 28 May–29 Aug 10–9:30; 19 Mar–27 May, 30 Aug–3 Nov 10–7; 5 Feb–18 Mar, 4 Nov–2 Jan 10:30–4:30 ✋ 1-, 2- and 5-day tickets: expensive. Bateaux Mouches: ✉ Port de la Conférence, Pont de l'Alma, Right Bank, 75008 ☎ 01 42 25 96 10; www.bateauxmouches.com 🕓 Daily, times vary. Also lunch and dinner cruises ✋ 70-minute cruise: moderate 🚇 Alma-Marceau, Franklin D. Roosevelt 🚌 28, 42, 49, 63, 72, 80, 83, 92. Canauxrama: ✉ Embark at Port de l'Arsenal, opposite 50 boulevard de la Bastille, 75012 or 13 Quai de la Loire, Bassin de la Villette, 75019 ☎ 01 42 39 15 00; www.canauxrama.com 🕓 Daily 9:45 and 2:45, reservations necessary Oct–Apr ✋ One-way 2.5hr trip: expensive. Arsenal: 🚇 Bastille 🚌 20, 29, 65, 86, 87, 91. Villette: 🚇 Jaurès 🚌 26, 48

Explore Montmartre: use the funicular up or down to Sacré-Cœur, or take the Montmartrobus from place Pigalle to place Jules Joffrin – the route criss-crosses itself, so it's worth going both ways. Both these cost one métro ticket each way. Or try the inexpensive Petit Train de Montmartre (tel: 01 42 62 24 00; www.promotrain.fr), departing every half-hour from place Blanche for a 40-minute ride with commentary and optional stop at place du Tertre.

Make for the beach: each summer Paris Plages ("Paris beaches") imports sand and palm trees. Lots of activities are on offer.
✉ Louvre to Pont de Sully, Pont de la Gare, Bassin de la Villette
☎ www.paris.fr ⏰ Opens about 20 Jul for 4 weeks, daily 8am–12am ✋ Free

Swimming: Paris has many pools both indoor and open-air. One of the newest is Piscine Josephine Baker floating off the Left Bank.
✉ Port de la Gare, quai François-Mauriac, 75013 ☎ 01 56 61 96 50; www.paris.fr ⏰ Daily, times vary 7am–11pm ✋ Inexpensive 🚇 Quai de la Gare, Bercy, Bibliothèque François Mitterrand 🚌 64, 89

Roller-skating rallies: anyone can join the three-hour mass skate.
✉ Place Raoul Dautry, 75015 ☎ www.pari-roller.com ⏰ Fri meet 9:30pm, depart 10pm (unless the streets are wet) 🚇 Montparnasse-Bienvenue
🚌 28, 58, 82, 91, 92, 94, 95, 96

2CV tours: these tours promise an "authentic" Paris experience, in Citroën 2CVs complete with beret-wearing driver-guides.
✉ Gregory's, place du Palais-Royal, 75011 ☎ 06 64 50 44 19; www.parisauthentic.com ⏰ By arrangement, basic tour 2 hours

Cycle-taxi: electric-assisted pedicabs such as Cyclobulle's serve the districts of Bastille, Louvre, Saint-Michel and Notre-Dame.
✉ Cyclobulle, 78 rue de Cléry, 75002 ☎ 01 42 36 58 43; www.cyclobulle.com ⏰ Mon–Sat 11–7 ✋ Guided tours: expensive

Segway tours: a wobble-free way to see the sights driving yourself on a two-wheeled, stand-up, gyroscopic machines.
✉ 24 rue Edgar Fauré, 75015 (meet at the south pillar of the Tour Eiffel)
☎ 01 56 58 10 54; www.citysegway.com ⏰ Mar–Nov 9:30 and 2, also Apr–Oct 6:30; Dec–Feb 9:30 ✋ Expensive 🚇 Bir-Hakiem 🚌 42, 69, 72, 82, 87

a walk

along the Seine and on the Islands

This relatively compact area offers stately historic buildings, breathtaking views, provincial charm and the liveliness of a great city.

Start from place du Châtelet on the Right Bank.

The monumental fountain was commissioned by Napoleon on his return from Egypt.

Walk along the quai de Gesvres, then across pont Notre-Dame.

The flower market on place Louis Lépine is a refreshing sight. On Sunday, flowers are replaced by birds.

Walk east along the embankment, turn right into rue des Ursins then left and left again.

The narrow streets of the medieval cathedral precinct have some old houses. At the tip of the island is an underground memorial to the victims of Nazi concentration camps.

Cross over to the Île St-Louis and turn left, following the quai de Bourbon.

Enjoy the peaceful atmosphere of this sought-after residential area.

Turn right into rue des Deux Ponts and cross over to the Left Bank. Walk west to square Viviani then cross rue St-Jacques into rue St-Séverin.

This is one of the oldest parts of the Quartier Latin. The Gothic church of St-Séverin has a magnificent interior.

From place St-Michel, cross back on to the Île de la Cité.

Sainte-Chapelle (► 93) is very close. Place Dauphine at the western end of the island is another haven of peace. Admire the view from pont Neuf, Paris's oldest bridge.

Cross over to the Right Bank and the Pont Neuf métro station.

Distance 4km (2.5 miles)
Time 2–4 hours depending on church visits
Start point Place du Châtelet ✚ 25P 🚇 Châtelet 🚌 21, 38, 47, 58, 70, 72, 74, 81, 85, 96
End point Pont Neuf ✚ 23P 🚇 Pont Neuf 🚌 21, 24, 27, 69, 72, 74, 75, 76, 81, 85, Balabus
Lunch L'Escale ✉ 1 rue des Deux-Ponts, 75004 ☎ 01 43 54 94, 23

Places to be entertained

CABARET AND MUSIC HALL
Le Lido
The show put on by the famous Bluebell girls is still very effective. It is possible to have dinner on a *bateau-mouche* followed by a show at the Lido.

✉ 116 bis avenue des Champs-Elysées, 75008 ☎ 01 40 76 56 10; www.lelido.fr Ⓜ George V 🚌 73

Moulin-Rouge
Undoubtedly the most famous of them all! The show still includes impressive displays of French can-can.

✉ 82 boulevard de Clichy, 75018 ☎ 01 53 09 82 82; www.moulinrouge.fr Ⓜ Blanche 🚌 30, 54, 68, 74

CONCERT VENUES
Cité de la Musique
This temple of all kinds of music – from classical to world to rock – regularly sets new trends with special commissions.

✉ 221 avenue Jean Jaurès, 75019 ☎ 01 44 84 44, 84; www.cite-musique.fr Ⓜ Porte de Pantin 🚌 75, N13, N41

Théâtre des Champs-Élysées
Paris's most prestigious classical concert venue hosting top international orchestras.

✉ 15 avenue Montaigne, 75008 ☎ 01 49 52 50 50; www.theatrechampselysees.fr Ⓜ Alma-Marceau, Franklin D. Roosevelt 🚌 42, 63, 72, 80, 92

Théâtre du Châtelet
Classical concerts, opera performances, ballets and variety shows alternate in this 19th-century theatre that has welcomed great names such as Mahler and Diaghilev.

✉ 1 place du Châtelet, 75001 ☎ 01 40 28 28 00; www.chatelet-theatre.com Ⓜ Châtelet 🚌 21, 38, 58, 67, 81, 85

JAZZ CLUBS

Caveau de la Huchette

Jazz and rock mania has been let loose in medieval cellars for more than 60 years.

✉ 5 rue de la Huchette, 75005 ☎ 01 43 26 65 05; www.caveaudelahuchette.fr Ⓜ Saint-Michel

Duc des Lombards

Many of the great names of jazz have played at this club-restaurant.

✉ 42 rue des Lombards, 75001 ☎ 01 42 33 22 88; www.ducdeslombards.com Ⓜ Châtelet 🚌 21, 38, 47, 58, 64, 67, 69, 70, 72, 74, 85, N11, N12, N13, N14, N15, N16, N120, N121, N122

Sunset-Sunside

The best jazz action has moved from St-Germain to the Right Bank where this double venue – Sunset dedicated to electric jazz and world music, Sunside to acoustic jazz – is the current Parisian favourite.

✉ 60 rue des Lombards, 75001 ☎ Sunset: 01 40 26 46 60; Sunside: 01 40 26 21 25; www.sunset-sunside.com Ⓜ Châtelet 🚌 21, 38, 47, 58, 64, 67, 69, 70, 72, 74, 85, N11, N12, N13, N14, N15, N16, N120, N121, N122

NIGHTCLUB

Le Favela Chic

There's a Latin-American carnival atmosphere in this nightclub cum restaurant with an eclectic music policy.

✉ 81 rue du Faubourg du Temple, 75011 ☎ 01 40 21 38 14; www.favelachic.com/paris Ⓜ République 🚌 20, 56, 65, 75, N142

Museums and art galleries

Grand Palais
The most strking feature of this centre with two galleries built for the World Exhibition of 1900, is its distinctive curved glass roof, especially when it is illuminated at night (➤ 119).

🚩 9K ✉ Galeries Nationales: avenue du Général Eisenhower, 75008; Palais de la Découverte, avenue Franklin D. Roosevelt, 75008 ☎ Galeries Nationales: 01 44 13 17 17; Palais de la Découverte: 01 56 43 20 20; www.grandpalais.fr 🚇 Champs-Elysées-Clemenceau 🚌 28, 32, 42, 72, 73, 80, 83, 93

Musée des Arts Décoratifs
This fascinating museum devoted to interior design and decoration has more than 150,000 items on display (➤ 122).

🚩 13L ✉ 107 rue de Rivoli, 75001 ☎ 01 44 55 57 50; www.lesartsdecoratifs.fr 🚇 Palais-Royal 🚌 21, 27, 39, 48, 68, 72, 81, 95

Musée Carnavalet
The Carnavalet retraces the history of Paris from antiquity to the present day, and is worth visiting for the buildings alone (➤ 143).

🚩 27P ✉ 23 rue de Sévigné, 75003 ☎ 01 44 59 58 58; www.carnavalet.paris.fr 🚇 Saint-Paul 🚌 29, 69, 76, 96

Musée Marmottan-Monet
Although off the beaten track, this is a must for anyone interested in the Impressionist movement and Monet in particular (➤ 123).

🚩 5L (off map) ✉ 2 rue Louis Boilly, 75016 ☎ 01 44 96 50 33; www.marmottan.com 🚇 La Muette 🚌 22, 32, 52, 63

Musée National du Moyen-Age
Medieval art is displayed in a 15th-century Gothic mansion, one of the last examples of medieval domestic architecture in Paris (➤ 90).

🚩 24Q ✉ 6 place Paul Painlevé, 75005 ☎ 01 53 73 78 00; 01 53 73 78 16; www.musee-moyenage.fr 🚇 Cluny-La Sorbonne, Saint-Michel, Odéon 🚌 21, 27, 38, 63, 85, 86, 87

Musée de l'Orangerie

Daylight enhances the magical appeal of Monet's monumental *nymphéas* (waterlilies) in rooms specifically designed to display them (➤ 124).

➕ 11L ✉ Jardin des Tuileries, 75001 ☎ 01 44 77 80 07; www.musee-orangerie.fr Ⓜ Concorde 🚌 24, 42, 52, 72, 73, 84, 94

Musée d'Orsay

Deservedly popular, this gallery of 19th- and early 20th-century art, featuring Impressionists and post-Impressionists in a magnificent former station on the banks of the Seine, is being rehung, but will remain open throughout the process, due to end in March 2011 (➤ 46–47).

➕ 12M ✉ 1 rue de la Légion d'Honneur, 75007 ☎ 01 40 49 48 14; www.musee-orsay.fr Ⓜ Solférino 🚌 24, 63, 68, 69, 73, 83, 84, 94
🚤 Batobus

Musée Rodin

One of the lovely mansions in the elegant Faubourg St-Germain, built by Gabriel in 1728, houses a unique collection of works by the sculptor Auguste Rodin (➤ 109).

➕ 19P ✉ 79 rue de Varenne, 75007 ☎ 01 44 18 61 10; www.musee-rodin.fr
Ⓜ Varenne, Invalides 🚌 69, 82, 87, 92

Palais de Chaillot

This imposing architectural complex overlooking the river and Tour Eiffel offers great views, three museums and a theatre (➤ 126). Together with other nearby cultural establishments it is known as La Colline des Musées (Museum Hill).

➕ 5L ✉ Place du Trocadéro, 75016 ☎ www.citechaillot.fr; Musée de l'Homme: 01 44 05 72 72; www.museedelhomme.fr; Musée Nationale de la Marine: 01 53 65 69 69; www.musee-marine.fr; Cité de l'architecture et du patrimoine: 01 58 51 52 00 Ⓜ Trocadéro, Iéna 🚌 22, 30, 32, 63, 72, 82
🚤 Batobus

Churches and cathedrals

Madeleine
This immense, neoclassical church, with its Corinthian pillars, is one of Paris's great landmarks (➤ 118).

➕ 11J ✉ Place de la Madeleine, 75008 ☎ 01 44 51 69 00 🚇 Madeleine
🚌 24, 42, 52, 84, 94

La Mosquée
A gem of 20th-century European Islamic architecture, with an impressive square minaret and ornate decoration.

➕ 25S ✉ Place du Puits-de-l'Ermite, 75005 ☎ 01 45 35 97 33;
www.mosquee-de-paris.org 🚇 Jussieu, Place Monge, Censier-Daubenton
🚌 47, 67, 89

Notre-Dame
The grandeur of this cathedral, one of the world's finest examples of early Gothic architecture, never fails to inspire (➤ 48–49).

➕ 25Q ✉ Place du Parvis Notre-Dame, 75004 ☎ 01 42 34 56 10;
www.cathedraledeparis.com 🚇 Cité, Saint-Michel 🚌 21, 24, 27, 38, 47, 85, 96

Sacré-Cœur, Basilique du
The gleaming white Basilica, at the top of Montmartre's hill, dominates the skyline, with views across the city (➤ 52–53).

➕ 3C ✉ Place du Parvis du Sacré-Cœur, 75018 ☎ 01 53 41 89 00;
www.sacre-coeur-montmartre.com 🚇 Abbesses (from here walk along rue Yvonne Le Tac, then take funicular or walk up steps) 🚌 30, 54, 85, Montmartrobus

Sainte-Chapelle
Sainte-Chapelle's stunning stained-glass windows make it one of Paris's most beautiful churches (➤ 93).

➕ 24P ✉ 8 boulevard du Palais, 75001 ☎ 01 53 40 60 80;
www.sainte-chapelle.monuments-nationaux.fr 🚇 Cité 🚌 21, 27, 38, 85, 96, Balabus

St-Etienne-du-Mont
This 15th-century church is an architectural mixture of Gothic
Flamboyant, Renaissance and Classical styles (➤ 92).
➕ 24R ✉ Place Ste-Geneviève, 75005 ☎ 01 43 54 11 79 Ⓜ Cardinal
Lemoine, Luxembourg 🚌 84, 89

St-Eustache
Paris's second-largest church after Notre-Dame took 105 years to
build. Henri de Miller's curious sculpture *L'Écoute*, stands outside
(➤ 140).
➕ 15L ✉ Rue du Jour, 75001 ☎ 01 42 36 31 05; www.saint-eustache.org
Ⓜ Les Halles 🚌 29, 67, 74, 85

St-Germain-des-Prés
At the heart of the lively district of St-Germain-des-Prés stands the
oldest church in Paris, dating back to the sixth century, the only
part of the original Benedictine abbey to survive the Revolution
(➤ 109).
➕ 22P ✉ Place St-Germain-des-Prés, 75006 ☎ 01 55 42 81 33;
www.eglise-sgp.org Ⓜ St-Germain-des-Prés 🚌 39, 63, 86, 95

St-Séverin
This Gothic church has a delightful blend of Flamboyant Gothic
architecture and beautiful stained glass (➤ 94).
➕ 24Q ✉ 1 rue des Prêtres-St-Séverin, 75005 ☎ 01 42 34 93 50;
www.saint-severin.com Ⓜ Saint-Michel, Cluny-La Sorbonne 🚌 21, 24, 27,
38, 47, 63, 85, 86, 87

St-Sulpice
The church and square of St-Sulpice form a harmonious
architectural ensemble, mostly dating from the 18th century, now
much visited by fans of Dan Brown's *The Da Vinci Code* (➤ 110).
➕ 22Q ✉ Place St-Sulpice, 75006 ☎ 01 46 33 21 78;
www.paroisse-saint-sulpice-paris.org Ⓜ St-Sulpice 🚌 63, 70, 84, 86, 87, 96

Places to stay

Four Seasons George V (€€€)

The George V offers the high levels of service you would
expect from an international hotel. Many of the guest
rooms have private balconies overlooking the city.

✉ 31 avenue George-V, 75008 ☎ 01 49 52 70 00;
www.fourseasons.com/paris 🚇 George V

Hôtel d'Angleterre Saint-Germain-des-Prés (€€–€€€)

The largest rooms of this quiet luxury hotel with an
illustrious history overlook the secluded garden.

✉ 44 rue Jacob, 75006 ☎ 01 42 60 34 72;
www.hotel-danleterre.com 🚇 St-Germain-des-Prés

Hôtel du Jeu de Paume (€€€)

Exclusive hotel on the Île St-Louis, housed in converted
Jeu de Paume (indoor tennis court), with striking galleries
and mezzanines.

✉ 54 rue Saint-Louis-en-l'Île, 75004 ☎ 01 43 26 14 18;
www.jeudepaumehotel.com 🚇 Pont Marie

Hôtel Mama Shelter (€€)

With DJs spinning until the early hours, this funky
destination hotel near Père Lachaise in the newly
fashionable 20th *arrondissement* is very popular with
clubbers.

✉ 109 rue de Bagnolet, 75020 ☎ 01 43 48 48 48;
www.mamashelter.com 🚇 Gambetta, Porte de Bagnolet

Hôtel Meurice (€€€)

The luxurious bedrooms at the historic Hotel Meurice,
overlooking the Jardin des Tuileries, are furnished with
antiques and the walls are hung with original paintings.

✉ 228 rue de Rivoli, 75001 ☎ 01 44 58 10 10; www.lemeurice.com
🚇 Tuileries, Concorde

Hôtel du Panthéon (€€–€€€)

An elegant hotel conveniently situated in the university district, with well-appointed air-conditioned bedrooms.

✉ 19 place du Panthéon, 75005 ☎ 01 43 54 32 95; www.hoteldupantheon.com 🚇 Cardinal Lemoine

Hôtel Place des Vosges (€)

Picturesque, quiet hotel just off the place des Vosges.

✉ 12 rue de Birague, 75004 ☎ 01 42 72 60 46; www.hotelplacedesvosges.com 🚇 Saint-Paul, Bastille

Hôtel Ritz Paris (€€€)

Sometimes called the palace of kings and the king of palaces, the Ritz shares with the Crillon the top of the list of Paris's luxury hotels. Overlooking the place Vendôme, it has a beautiful swimming pool and luxury fitness centre; prices are accordingly very high.

✉ 15 place Vendôme, 75001 ☎ 01 43 16 30 30; www.ritzparis.com 🚇 Opéra

Hôtel Secret de Paris (€€–€€€)

Boutique hotel with its own hammam, wittily decorated on the theme of the great landmarks of Paris. The Musée d'Orsay room has its big clock at the head of the bed, while the Moulin Rouge has a carpet of red roses.

✉ 2 rue de Parme, 75009 ☎ 01 53 16 33 33; www.hotelsecretdeparis.com 🚇 Clichy, Blanche

Pavillon de la Reine (€€€)

In one of the two royal pavilions of the place des Vosges, this luxury hotel has air-conditioned rooms which overlook its own courtyard or garden, and a spa with hamman.

✉ 28 Place des Vosges, 75003 ☎ 01 40 29 19 19; www.pavillon-de-la-reine.com 🚇 Bastille

Best shopping

Au Printemps
Three stores in one: Le Printemps de la Mode for fashion; Le Printemps de la Beauté et Maison for the world's largest beauty department and elegant homeware, and a separate building, devoted to menswear. Don't miss the rooftop restaurant.
✉ 64 boulevard Haussmann, 75009 ☎ 01 42 82 50 00; www.printemps.com
🚇 Havre-Caumartin

BHV
Le Bazar de l'Hôtel de Ville has fashion and homewares (menswear and pets are in nearby buildings) but is chiefly remarkable for its huge do-it-yourself department in the basement.
✉ 55 rue de la Verrerie (also entrances on rue de Rivoli opposite Hôtel de Ville), 75004 ☎ 01 42 74 90 00; www.bhv.fr 🚇 Hôtel de Ville

Le Bon Marché Rive Gauche
The only department store on the Left Bank, and the oldest in Paris, opened in 1838. It specializes in chic homeware and fashion. Don't miss its haberdashery and designer furniture departments.
✉ 24 rue de Sèvres, 75007 ☎ 01 44 39 80 00, www.lebonmarche.com
🚇 Sèvres-Babylone

Boulangerie Poîlane
The most famous bakery in Paris. Long queues form outside this shop for the traditionally baked bread.
✉ 8 rue du Cherche-Midi, 75006 ☎ 01 45 48 42 59; www.poilane.fr
🚇 Sèvres-Babylone

Fauchon and Hédiard
Strictly for gourmets! Two luxury delicatessens with high-quality French regional products.
✉ Fauchon at No 26, Hédiard at No 21 place de la Madeleine, 75008
☎ Fauchon: 01 70 39 38 00; www.fauchon.com Hédiard: 01 43 12 88 88; www.hediard.fr 🚇 Madeleine

Galeries Lafayette

In an enchanting belle époque building under a giant glass dome, you'll find fashion, homewares and gifts, and an enormous shoe department.

✉ 40 boulevard Haussmann, 75009 ☎ 01 42 82 34 56; www.galerieslafayette.com
🚇 Chaussée d'Antin

Marché Saint-Germain

Fashion and gift shops including leather goods, perfume and jewellery.

✉ Rue Clément, 75006 🚇 Mabillon

Monoprix

The good-value French supermarket chain, selling clothes, toys, household necessities, food and wine.

✉ 52 avenue des Champs-Elysées, 75008
☎ 01 53 77 65 65; www.monoprix.fr
🚇 Franklin D. Roosevelt

Shakespeare & Company

This English bookshop has become a legend. New and second-hand books.

✉ 37 rue de la Bûcherie, 75005 ☎ 01 43 26 96 50 🚇 Maubert-Mutualité

Tati

Clothes at absurdly inexpensive prices. A French institution.

✉ 68 avenue du Maine, 75014 ☎ 01 56 80 06 80; www.tati.fr 🚇 Gaîté, Montparnasse-Bienvenue, Edgar Quinet

Exploring

The city of Paris has always played its role of capital of France to the full. It is where the French nation's future is decided, where revolutions began in the past and where major political, economic and social changes are traditionally launched. This is as true today as it ever was, in spite of many attempts at decentralization.

Parisian life reflects the city's leading role in many different ways: the numerous trade exhibitions and international conferences taking place every year testify to its economic and political dynamism and healthy competitive spirit. Paris is continually on the move in all fields of human activity: its architectural heritage is constantly expanding and it is proudly setting new trends in the arts, in gastronomy and in fashion. Paris is also a cosmopolitan metropolis where many ethnic groups find the necessary scope to express their differences.

The Latin Quarter and the Islands

Situated on the Left Bank between the Carrefour de l'Odéon and the Jardin des Plantes, the lively Latin Quarter was known in medieval times as the "Montagne Ste-Geneviève" after the patron saint of Paris, and was later given the name of "Quartier Latin" because Latin was spoken at the university until the late 18th century. To this day it remains the undisputed kingdom of Parisian students. The Sorbonne, the most famous French university

college, was founded in 1257; the present building dates from the late 19th century when well-known artists such as Puvis de Chavannes decorated the interior. The adjacent 17th-century church is a model of Jesuit style.

The two river islands – Île de la Cité and Île St-Louis – have very different histories and characters. The Île de la Cité is not only the historic centre of Paris, it is also a place of exceptional natural beauty and home to three major monuments – Notre-Dame, Sainte-Chapelle and the Conciergerie. The peaceful atmosphere of the Île St-Louis is apparent as soon as you walk along its shaded embankment, lined with elegant 17th-century mansions that stand as silent witnesses of a bygone era.

BIBLIOTHÈQUE NATIONALE DE FRANCE: FRANÇOIS MITTERRAND

These four impressive towers in the shape of open books became the new home of France's national library in 1996 and are at the centre of a rapidly regenerating part of Paris. Cutting-edge art galleries, more at home to conceptual art and installations than paintings, cluster in nearby streets, especially rue Louise Weiss; **Les Frigos,** an old refrigeration plant now given over to artists' studios, lends a stamp of scruffy authenticity; and a new centre devoted to fashion and design, the **Cité de la Mode et du Design,** housed in old industrial buildings with a daring modern architectural overlay, is due to open late in 2010. A *passerelle*, or footbridge, named after the feminist Simone de Beauvoir, swoops across the Seine to link the library with the Cinémathèque (➤ 144) at Bercy on the Right Bank.

www.bnf.fr

🚻 28T off map ✉ Quai François-Mauriac, 75013 ☎ 01 53 79 40 43
🕐 Tue–Sat 10–7, Sun 1–9 💷 Temporary exhibitions: moderate
🚇 Bibliothèque François-Mitterrand 🚌 62, 64, 89

Les Frigos

🚻 28T off map ✉ 19 rue des Frigos, 75013 ☎ www.les-frigos.com
🕐 Open studios at various times; visits to individual artists' studios by appointment only 🚇 Bibliothèque François-Mitterrand
🚌 62, 64, 89

Cité de la Mode et du Design

🚻 28T ✉ 26, quai d'Austerlitz, 75013 🕐 Due to open late 2010
🚇 Gare d'Austerlitz 🚌 89

LES CATACOMBS

Many centuries-old tunnels run under Paris, left by excavations for building stone, gypsum and clay. By the 18th century, the city's church graveyards were dangerously full and began to spread disease. So from 1786 the graves were emptied and the remains brought here to be reinterred 20m (66ft) – and 130 steps down, 83 steps up – below ground. Cartloads of the dead crossed Paris by night, covered in black cloth and accompanied by chanting priests. The clearances continued until the beginning of the 20th century, but from the start the catacombs were a fashionable place to visit. Many millions of Parisians were reburied here anonymously but we know that among the famous bones are those of the great actor Scaramouche, Louis XV's mistress Madame de Pompadour, hundreds of revolutionaries, the writer Rabelais, Lavoisier, founder of the metric system, and the Man in the Iron Mask, whose identity is a secret to this day.

www.catacombes-de-paris.fr

🚇 23T off map ✉ 1 avenue du Colonel Henri Rol-Tanguy, 75014 ☎ 01 43 22 47 63 🕐 Tue–Sun 10–5 (last entry 4pm) ✋ Moderate 🚇 Denfert-Rocherau 🚌 38, 68 ❓ No toilets, no lift, not recommended for those with heart conditions or small children; guided tours by appointment, tel: 01 44 59 58 32

CITÉ, ÎLE DE LA

The Celtic tribe the Parisii settled on the largest island in an area known as Lutetia, which under the Romans expanded onto the Left Bank of the Seine. Nevertheless, the island (the Cité), which the king of the Franks, Clovis, chose as his capital in AD 508, remained for 1,000 years the seat of royal, judicial and religious power. During the Middle Ages, the Île de la Cité was an important intellectual centre as its cathedral schools attracted students from all over Europe. Even after the kings of France left the royal palace for larger premises on the Right Bank, the Cité lost none of its symbolic importance and remains to this day the "guardian" of 2,000 years of history.

The appearance of the Cité has changed considerably over the years; in the 19th century, the centre of the island was cleared and the vast square in front of Notre-Dame Cathedral created. At the other end of the island, the Conciergerie and Sainte-Chapelle are the only remaining parts of the medieval royal palace, now incorporated in the huge Palais de Justice.

➕ 25P ✉ Île de la Cité, 75001 and 75004 🍴 Restaurants and cafés (€–€€) on the island and on the Right and Left banks 🚇 Cité, Pont Neuf, Saint-Michel, Châtelet, Hôtel de Ville 🚌 21, 24, 27, 38, 47, 58, 67, 69, 70, 72, 74, 75, 76, 85, 96, Balabus 🚢 Batobus

LA CONCIERGERIE

For most people, the name "Conciergerie" suggests crowds of innocent prisoners waiting to be taken to the guillotine. Nowadays, its familiar round towers covered with conical slate roofs and the square clock tower, which housed the first public clock in Paris, are one of the most picturesque sights of the Île de la Cité. The Conciergerie is the last remaining authentic part of a 14th-century royal complex, administered by a *concierge* or governor. The twin towers marked the main entrance to the palace. In the late 14th century, the Conciergerie was turned into a prison but it only acquired a sinister reputation during the Revolution, when it held a number of famous prisoners, including Queen Marie-Antoinette, Madame du Barry and the poet André Chénier, as well as Danton and Robespierre. The visit includes the original guards' room, a magnificent great hall with Gothic vaulting and kitchens with monumental fireplaces. There is also a reconstruction of Marie-Antoinette's cell.

www.conciergerie.monuments-nationaux.fr

➕ 24P ✉ 2 boulevard du Palais, 75001 ☎ 01 53 40 60 97 🕐 Mar–Oct daily 9:30–6; Nov–Feb 9:30–5. Closed 1 Jan, 1 May, 25 Dec ✋ Moderate 🚇 St-Michel, Cité, Châtelet 🚌 21, 24, 27, 38, 58, 81, 85, 96, Balabus ❓ Guided tours, bookshop

INSTITUT DU MONDE ARABE

The Institute of Arab and Islamic Civilization is a remarkable piece of modern architecture designed by the French architect Jean Nouvel. Its glass-and-aluminium facade, reminiscent of a

musharabia (carved wooden screen), discreetly refers to Arab tradition. The seventh floor houses a museum of Islamic art and civilization from the eighth century to the present day. The ninth floor offers a panoramic view of the Île de la Cité and Île St-Louis.

www.imarabe.org

➕ 26R ✉ 1 rue des Fossés St-Bernard, 75005 ☎ 01 40 51 38 38 🕐 Tue, Wed, Fri 10–6, Thu 10–10, Sat–Sun 10–8. Closed 1 May. Museum partly closed for renovation until late 2011 ✋ Moderate 🍴 Restaurant (€–€€) 🚇 Jussieu, Cardinal Lemoine, Sully-Morland 🚌 24, 63, 67, 86, 87, 89 ❓ Guided tours, shops

MOYEN-AGE, MUSÉE NATIONAL DU

This museum, also known as the Musée de Cluny, stands at the heart of the Quartier Latin, on the site of Gallo-Roman baths dating from the third century AD. The ruins are surrounded by a public garden. Inside the main courtyard, the elegant stair tower and corner turrets are particularly noteworthy.

 All the arts and crafts of the medieval period are illustrated, the most famous exhibit being a set of tapestries known as "La Dame à la Licorne", made in a Brussels workshop at the end of the 15th century. There is also an exceptionally fine collection of sculptures, including the heads of the kings of Judaea that decorated the facade of Notre-Dame cathedral and were knocked down during the Revolution.

www.musee-moyenage.fr

✚ 24Q ✉ 6 place Paul Painlevé, 75005 ☎ 01 53 73 78 00; 01 53 73 78 16
🕐 Wed–Mon 9:15–5:45. Closed 1 Jan, 1 May, 25 Dec 👋 Moderate; free 1st Sun of month 🍴 Boulevard St-Michel nearby (€–€€) 🚇 Cluny-La Sorbonne
🚌 21, 27, 38, 63, 85, 86, 87 ❓ Guided tours, shops, concerts

NOTRE-DAME

Best places to see, ➤ 48–49.

PANTHÉON

Commissioned by Louis XV, the building was meant to replace St Genevieve's Church in the Quartier Latin; designed by Soufflot, who gave it the shape of a Greek cross surmounted by a high dome it is now one of Paris's landmarks. Completed on the eve of the Revolution, it became a Pantheon for France's illustrious dead, among them Voltaire, Rousseau, Hugo, Zola, and more recently Jean Moulin (head of the French Resistance during World War II) and André Malraux (writer and successful Minister of Culture).

www.pantheon.monuments-nationaux.fr

✚ 24R ✉ Place du Panthéon, 75005 ☎ 01 44 32 18 00 🕐 Apr–Sep daily 10–6:30; Oct–Mar 10–6. Closed 1 Jan, 1 May, 25 Dec 🎫 Moderate 🚇 Maubert-Mutualité, Cardinal Lemoine 🚌 21, 27, 38, 82, 84, 85, 89 ❓ Shops

LA CONVENTION NATIONALE

PLANTES, JARDIN DES

The botanical gardens form the experimental gardens of the Muséum National d'Histoire Naturelle (Natural History Museum) and make an ideal spot for a leisurely stroll; children love the *ménagerie* (zoo). There are also hothouses, an alpine garden and several exhibition halls, the most fascinating being the Grande Galerie de l'Évolution, illustrating the evolution of life on Earth and Man's influence on it. Also featured are scientists associated with evolution and the latest discoveries in the field of genetics.
www.mnhn.fr

🚪 27S 📧 57 rue Cuvier, 75005 ☎ 01 40 79 54 79; 01 40 79 56 01
🕐 Gardens: daily 8–dusk (summer 7:30am–8pm). Museum: Wed–Mon 10–6. Zoo: summer daily 9–6; winter 9–5 ✋ Gardens: free; museum and zoo: moderate 🍴 Cafeteria (€) 🚇 Gare d'Austerlitz, Jussieu, Censier-Daubenton
🚌 24, 57, 61, 63, 67, 89, 91 ⛴ Batobus ❓ Lectures, exhibitions, workshops for children, shop

LES QUAIS

Best places to see, ➤ 50–51.

ST-ETIENNE-DU-MONT

The Church of St-Etienne-du-Mont, dating from the late 15th century, combines Flamboyant Gothic and Renaissance styles. Don't miss the delicately fretted rood-screen inside.

🚪 24R 📧 Place Ste-Geneviève, 75005 ☎ 01 43 54 11 79 🕐 Tue–Fri 8:45–7:30, Sat–Sun 8:45–12:15, 2:30–7:45 ✋ Free 🚇 Cardinal Lemoine, Luxembourg 🚌 84, 89

SAINTE-CHAPELLE

The full splendour of this magnificent Gothic chapel, surely Paris's most beautiful church, can only be appreciated from inside, as Sainte-Chapelle is closely surrounded by the Palais de Justice buildings. Commissioned by Louis IX, a king so devout that he came to be known as Saint Louis, to house the Crown of Thorns and a fragment of the true Cross, it was built in less than three years by Pierre de Montreuil and was consecrated in 1248.

The building, which remains open during extensive renovations, consists of two chapels, the lower one intended to serve as a parish church for the palace staff and the upper chapel, which was reserved for the royal family. The latter is a striking example of architectural and technical prowess: walls have been replaced by 15m-high (49ft) stained-glass panels linked by slender pillars which also support the fine vaulting. The stained-glass windows, which cover an area of more than 600sq m (6,460sq ft), are mainly original and illustrate scenes from the Old and New Testaments.

www.sainte-chapelle.monuments-nationaux.fr

🕂 24P ✉ 4 boulevard du Palais, 75001 ☎ 01 53 40 60 97 🕐 Mar–Oct daily 9:30–6; Nov–Feb 9–5. Closed 1 Jan, 1 May, 1 Nov 🖐 Moderate 🚇 Cité 🚌 21, 27, 38, 85, 96, Balabus ❓ Shop

ST-LOUIS, ÎLE

The island was formed at the beginning of the 17th century, when two small islands were united and joined to the mainland by a couple of bridges linked by the rue des Deux Ponts, which still exists; at the same time, private residences were built along the embankment and the straight narrow streets. The whole project was completed in a remarkably short time between 1627 and 1664. Since then, time seems to have stood still on the Île St-Louis, which retains its sleepy character.

A few architectural gems can be seen along quai de Bourbon and quai d'Anjou, which offer fine views of the Right Bank. From the western tip of the island you can see Notre-Dame and the Île de la Cité. Concerts are regularly given in the classical church of St-Louis-en-l'Île, richly decorated inside.

✚ 26Q ✉ 75004 🍴 Rue St-Louis-en-l'Île (€€) Ⓜ Pont Marie 🚌 67, 86, 87, Balabus

ST-SÉVERIN

St-Séverin is one of the most beautiful churches in the capital, with its delightful blend of Flamboyant Gothic architecture and contemporary stained glass. It dates originally from the 13th century and is dedicated to the sixth-century hermit St Séverin, who was closely associated with St Martin, patron saint of travellers. The surrounding cobbled streets, full of cafés, shops and inexpensive eateries, are popular with students and visitors alike.

www.saint-severin.com

✚ 24Q ✉ 1 rue des Prêtres-St-Séverin, 75005 ☎ 01 42 34 93 50
🕐 Mon–Sat 11–7:30, Sun 9–8:30 Ⓜ Saint-Michel, Cluny-La Sorbonne
🚌 21, 24, 27, 38, 47, 63, 85, 86, 87, 96, Balabus

HOTELS

Hôtel Esmeralda (€€€)

Some rooms in this old-fashioned yet cosy hotel offer delightful
views of Notre-Dame. Beware – no lift!

✉ 4 rue Saint-Julien-le-Pauvre, 75005 ☎ 01 43 54 19 20;
www.hotel-esmeralda.fr 🚇 Saint-Michel

Hôtel des Grandes Écoles (€€)

This oasis of peace in the Latin Quarter has the advantage of its
own garden. Rooms are decorated in elegant country style.

✉ 75 rue Cardinal Lemoine, 75005 ☎ 01 43 26 79 23;
www.hotel-grandes-ecoles.com 🚇 Cardinal Lemoine, Place Monge

L'Hôtel Hospitel (€€)

Simple rooms in one of the city's more unusual places to stay – on
the sixth floor of the oldest hospital in Paris, next to Notre Dame.

✉ Hôtel-Dieu, 1 place du Parvis Notre Dame, 75004 ☎ 01 44 32 01 00;
www.hotel-hospitel.com 🚇 Cité, Saint-Michel

Hôtel du Jeu de Paume (€€€)

See page 78.

Hôtel du Panthéon (€€)

See page 79.

Hôtel Les Rives de Notre-Dame (€€–€€€)

Elegant and comfortable, with soundproofed bedrooms, this hotel
has a lovely view overlooking the quai Saint-Michel and the Île de
la Cité.

✉ 15 quai Saint-Michel, 75005 ☎ 01 43 54 81 16;
www.rivesdenotredame.com 🚇 Saint-Michel

Hôtel des Trois Collèges (€–€€)

Roof beams and dormer windows add a picturesque touch to
this simple yet comfortable hotel close to the Sorbonne.

✉ 16 rue Cujas, 75005 ☎ 01 43 54 67 30; www.3colleges.com
🚇 Cluny-La Sorbonne

Odéon Hôtel (€€)

The 18th-century building, with its stone facade and exposed beams, exudes an old-world charm but the comfort is definitely 21st-century, with air-conditioning and broadband internet access.

✉ 3 rue de l'Odéon, 75006 ☎ 01 43 25 90 67; www.odeonhotel.fr

🚇 Odéon

Relais St-Jacques (€€€)

This small hotel offers 23 comfortable, individually styled rooms, close to the Luxembourg Gardens.

✉ 3 rue de l'Abbé de l'Epée, 75005 ☎ 01 53 73 26 00; www.relais-saint-jacques.com 🚇 Luxembourg

Résidence les Gobelins (€)

A haven of peace near the lively rue Mouffetard; warm welcome.

✉ 9 rue des Gobelins, 75013 ☎ 01 47 07 26 90; www.hotelgobelins.com

🚇 Les Gobelins

Select Hôtel (€€)

This fully modernized hotel in the heart of the Latin Quarter, close to the Luxembourg Gardens, has retained its stone walls and exposed beams; intimate atmosphere; glass-roofed patio.

✉ 1 place de la Sorbonne, 75005 ☎ 01 46 34 14 80; www.selecthotel.fr

🚇 Cluny-La Sorbonne, Odéon

RESTAURANTS

L'Atelier Maître Albert (€€)

A modern rotisserie and one of chef Guy Savoy's restaurants. Light, contemporary cuisine, elegant decoration.

✉ 1 rue Maître Albert, 75005 ☎ 01 56 81 30 01; www.ateliermaitrealbert.com

🕐 Mon–Fri lunch, dinner; Sat, Sun dinner only 🚇 Maubert-Mutualité, Saint-Michel

Brasserie Balzar (€€)

Stylish brasserie close to the Sorbonne, serving French dishes.

✉ 49 rue des Écoles, 75005 ☎ 01 43 54 13 67; www.brasseriebalzar.com

🕐 Daily 12–11:30 🚇 Cluny-La Sorbonne

Brasserie de l'Île Saint-Louis (€€)

The *choucroute garnie* (sauerkraut with sausage) is excellent, as is the onion tart. Leave room for dessert.

✉ 55 quai de Bourbon, 75004 ☎ 01 43 54 02 59 🕐 Thu–Tue 12–11:30 🚇 Pont Marie

La Criée (€)

For lovers of seafood at affordable prices! One branch of a small, nationwide chain.

✉ 15 rue Lagrange, 75005 ☎ 01 43 54 23 57; www.lacriee.com 🕐 Lunch, dinner 🚇 Maubert-Mutualité

Mavrommatis (€–€€)

Refined traditional Greek cuisine; alfresco dining in summer.

✉ 42 rue Daubenton, 75005 ☎ 01 43 31 17 17; www.mavrommatis.fr 🕐 Thu–Sun lunch, Tue–Sat dinner; closed Mon 🚇 Censier-Daubenton

Mon Vieil Ami (€€)

Trendy rustic decoration; delicious, reasonably priced dishes with vegetables given pride of place.

✉ 69 rue Saint-Louis-en-l'Île, 75004 ☎ 01 40 46 01 35; www.mon-vieil-ami.com 🕐 Lunch, dinner; closed Mon and Tue 🚇 Pont Marie

Nos Ancêtres les Gaulois (€€)

Convivial atmosphere in a 17th-century setting; the menu includes as much wine as you can drink.

✉ 39 rue St-Louis-en-l'Île, 75004 ☎ 01 46 33 66 07; www.nosancetreslesgaulois.com 🕐 Daily 7pm–1:30am 🚇 Pont Marie

Le Reminet (€–€€)

Refined bistro-style fare; terrace in summer. Extraordinarily good desserts. Friendly service.

✉ 3 rue des Grands-Degrés, 75005 ☎ 01 44 07 04 24; www.lereminet.com 🕐 Lunch, dinner 🚇 Saint-Michel, Cluny-La Sorbonne, Maubert-Mutualité

La Tour d'Argent (€€€)

See page 63.

La Truffière (€€€)

Very refined cuisine served in pleasant surroundings. The menu makes good use of truffles, as the name suggests.

✉ 4 rue Blainville, 75005 ☎ 01 46 33 29 82; www.la-truffiere.fr 🕐 Lunch, dinner; closed Sun, Mon 🚇 Place Monge, Cardinal Lemoine

SHOPPING

ART, ANTIQUES AND HANDICRAFTS

La Tuile à Loup

Handicrafts from various French regions.

✉ 35 rue Daubenton, 75005 ☎ 01 47 07 28 90; www.latuilealoup.com
🚇 Censier-Daubenton

BOOKS, CDs AND DVDs

The Abbey Bookshop

New and second-hand books from Britain, Canada and the USA.

✉ 29 rue de la Parcheminerie, 75005 ☎ 01 46 33 16 24 🚇 Saint-Michel

Gibert Joseph

A favourite haunt of the student population – books, CDs and DVDs.

✉ 26–34 boulevard St-Michel, 75006 ☎ 01 44 41 88 88;
www.gilbertjoseph.com 🚇 Saint-Michel

Librairie Ulysse

New and second-hand books, maps and magazines from around the world in a congenial atmosphere.

✉ 26 rue Saint-Louis-en-l'Île, 75004 ☎ 01 43 25 17 35; www.ulysse.fr
🚇 Sully-Morland

Shakespeare & Company

See page 81.

FOOD AND WINES

Berthillon

Mouth-watering ice cream in a wide range of flavours.

✉ 29–31 rue Saint-Louis-en-l'Île, 75004 ☎ 01 43 54 31 61; www.berthillon.fr
🕐 Closed Mon and Tue 🚇 Pont Marie

La Ferme St-Aubin

Delicious French and European cheeses, all in peak condition.

✉ 76 rue Saint-Louis en l'Île, 75004 ☎ 01 43 54 74 54 🕐 Closed Mon
🚇 Pont Marie

MARKETS
Marché aux Fleurs

Picturesque daily market (8–7) that becomes a bird market on
Sundays (8–7).

✉ Place Louis Lépine, Île de la Cité, 75004 🚇 Cité

Rue Mouffetard

A lively narrow road where shops spill onto the street, with some
stalls at the place Saint-Médard end. Not an official street market,
though there is a proper food market nearby at place Monge.

✉ Rue Mouffetard, 75005 🕐 Marché Monge: Wed, Fri, Sun 7–2:30
🚇 Place Monge, Censier-Daubenton

ENTERTAINMENT

CABARET
Paradis Latin (€€€)

Dinner followed by a live cabaret.

✉ 28 rue du Cardinal Lemoine, 75005 ☎ 01 43 25 28 28;
www.paradis-latin.com 🕐 Closed Tue 🚇 Cardinal Lemoine

CINEMA
Studio Galande

Shows such cult offerings as *The Rocky Horror Show* on Fridays
and Saturdays, with art films and cartoons during the week.

✉ 42 rue Galande, 75005 ☎ 01 43 54, 72, 71; www.studiogalande.fr
🚇 Saint-Michel

DANCE CLUB
Le Saint

Small dance club offering a range of music to suit most tastes.

✉ 7 rue St-Séverin, 75005 ☎ 01 40 20 43 23; www.lesaintdisco.com
🚇 Saint-Michel

JAZZ CLUBS
Caveau de la Huchette
See page 73.

Le Caveau des Oubliettes
Cool jazz in a medieval cellar – with its own guillotine.
✉ 52 rue Galande, 75005 ☎ 01 46 34 23 09; www.caveaudesoubliettes.fr
🚇 Saint-Michel

NIGHTCLUBS AND BARS
Le Batofar
A floating institution moored on the Left Bank, this boat has an
eclectic music policy ranging from rock and pop to dub and techno.
✉ Opposite 11 quai François Mauriac, 75013 ☎ www.batofar.org 🚇 Quai
de la Gare, Bibliothèque François-Mitterrand

La Dame de Canton
Dinner and a DJ or live music on a Chinese junk on the Left Bank.
✉ Port de la Gare, 75013 ☎ 01 53 61 08 49; www.damedecanton.com
🕐 Tue–Sat, from 8 🚇 Quai de la Gare, Bibliothèque François-Mitterrand

Zed Club
Rock, jazz, swing, salsa and 1960s–1990s pop.
✉ 2 rue des Anglais, 75005 ☎ 01 43 54 93 78 🕐 Thu–Sat nights
🚇 Maubert-Mutalité

SPORT
Club Quartier Latin
Fitness club with swimming pool, squash court, sauna.
✉ 19 rue de Pontoise, 75005 ☎ 01 55 42 77 88; www.clubquartierlatin.com
🚇 Maubert-Mutualité

THEATRE
Théâtre de la Huchette
A Parisian institution, with performances of works by Ionesco.
✉ 23 rue de la Huchette, 75005 ☎ 01 43 26 38 99;
www.theatrehuchette.com 🚇 Saint-Michel

Eiffel Tower to St-Germain-des-Prés

The Rive Gauche (Left Bank), with its narrow streets lined with shops and restaurants, and its breathtaking monuments, exudes Parisian charm. It's one of the most sought-after residential districts in Paris and eternally magnetic to both visitors and residents.

The Left Bank in this chapter comprises the area from the Tour Eiffel in the west to the Jardin du Luxembourg in the east, and south to include Montparnasse, a district popular with artists and writers in the early years of the 20th century. Some of the city's best-known attractions are found on the Left Bank – the Musée d'Orsay, housed in a magnificent Industrial Age railway terminus, the atmospheric Quartier St-Germain-des-Prés, with its many literary associations, the imposing architectural ensemble of Les Invalides, and that marvel of 19th-century engineering, the Eiffel Tower.

INVALIDES

ST GERMAIN-DES-PRÉS

MONTPARNASSE

ASSEMBLÉE NATIONALE PALAIS-BOURBON

The facade of this neoclassical building, where the lower house of the French parliament sits, echoes that of the Madeleine across the place de la Concorde. Completed by Louis XV's architect Gabriel, the Palais-Bourbon still bears the name of the French royal family to whom it once belonged. Guided tours (identity document required) include the chamber, where the 577 *deputés*, or members of parliament, sit on benches arranged in semicircular tiers, several reception rooms and the library, richly decorated by Delacroix.

www.assemblee-nationale.fr

➕ 10L ✉ 33 quai d'Orsay, 75007 ☎ 01 40 63 60 00
🕐 Guided tours by appointment. Closed public hols and when Parliament is sitting 👆 Free 🚇 Assemblée Nationale
🚌 24, 63, 73, 83, 84, 93, 94 ❓ Shops

EUGÈNE DELACROIX, MUSÉE NATIONAL

The old-world charm of the tiny rue de Furstenberg, hidden behind the church of St-Germain-des-Prés, is the perfect setting for a museum devoted to one of the major French Romantic painters. Delacroix lived and worked here from 1857 until the end of his life in 1863. Besides a few paintings, the house and the studio he built in the garden are full of mementoes of the artist, letters, sketches...and his palette. There is also a bookshop. It is well worth taking time to explore the picturesque neighbourhood.

www.musee-delacroix.fr

➕ 22P ✉ 6 rue de Furstenberg, 75006 ☎ 01 44 41 86 50
🕐 Wed–Mon 9:30–5. Closed public hols 👆 Inexpensive
🚇 St-Germain-des-Prés, Mabillon 🚌 39, 63, 70, 86, 95, 96

FAUBOURG ST-GERMAIN

This "suburb" is today one of the most elegant districts of central Paris. Its name came from the nearby Abbaye de St-Germain-des-Prés to which it belonged in medieval times. University students loved to stroll through the meadows stretching down to the river west of the abbey and the area remained in its natural state until the 18th century, when it became fashionable for the aristocracy and the wealthy middle class to have mansions built there by the fashionable architects of the time.

In the rue de Varenne you will find the Hôtel Matignon, now the prime minister's residence, and the Hôtel Biron, better known as the Musée Rodin (➤ 109). The parallel rue de Grenelle is interesting for its wealth of authentic architecture, including the Hôtel de Villars, now the town hall of the 7th *arrondissement*. Farther along, on the opposite side at No 61, is an interesting museum devoted to the sculptor Maillol (➤ 106).

✠ 22P ✉ 75007 ⌚ For the museums' opening times, see the relevant entries 🍴 Cafés and restaurants nearby in boulevard St-Germain (€–€€) Ⓜ Varenne, Rue du Bac 🚌 63, 69, 83, 84, 94

LES INVALIDES

Best places to see, ➤ 42–43.

JEAN MOULIN, MUSÉE

Sharing premises and a common aim with the Mémorial Leclerc et de la Libération de Paris, the Musée Jean Moulin tells the wider story of France in World War II through the life of one of its heroes. Parachuting into France more than once after meeting General de Gaulle in London, Resistance leader Jean Moulin was captured by the Nazis in Lyon and died after being interrogated by Klaus Barbie, head of the Gestapo there, without revealing anything.

A general during the war, Marshal Philippe Leclerc de Hauteclocque joined the Free French forces after the fall of

France in 1940 and fought in West Africa. His 2nd Armoured Division then landed in Normandy before going on to liberate Paris. His life and wartime activities are commemorated in a museum.

www.ml-leclerc-moulin.paris.fr

✚ 20T ✉ 23 allée de la 2e DB, Jardin Atlantique (on top of Montparnasse mainline station), 75015 ☎ 01 40 64 39 44 ⏱ Tue–Sun 10–6 ✋ Inexpensive Ⓜ Montparnasse-Bienvenüe, Gaîté, Pasteur 🚌 28, 58, 88, 91, 92, 94, 95, 96 ❓ From Montparnasse mainline station, take the staircase on the left of TGV platform 3; or, outside the station, elevators from rue du Cdt René Mouchotte or boulevard de Vaugirard

LUXEMBOURG, JARDIN DU

This French-style garden is traditionally the haunt of students and lovers, who favour the area surrounding the Fontaine de Médicis, named after Marie de Médicis, who commissioned the Palais du Luxembourg (now the Senate) and the gardens.

🚇 22R ✉ Rue de Médicis, rue de Vaugirard, boulevard St-Michel, 75006 ☎ 01 42 34 23 62 🕐 Daily 7:30 or 8–dusk 🚇 Luxembourg 🚌 21, 27, 38, 58, 82, 83, 84, 85, 89

MAILLOL, MUSÉE

This attractive museum displays many works by French painter and sculptor Aristide Maillol (1861–1944), as well as a private collection of works by Ingres, Cézanne, Matisse, Degas, Gauguin, Picasso, Rodin and Kandinsky among others. Maillol's theme was the nude: some of his rounded figures can be seen in the Jardin des Tuileries. **www.**museemaillol.com

🚇 20P ✉ 61 rue de Grenelle, 75007 ☎ 01 42 22 59 58 🕐 Wed–Mon 11–6. Closed public hols ♿ Moderate 🍴 Cafeteria (€) 🚇 Rue du Bac 🚌 63, 68, 69, 83, 84, 94 ❓ Shop

MONTPARNASSE

In the early 20th century, young artists and writers left Montmartre to settle on the Left Bank, in Montparnasse. Modigliani, Chagall, Léger and many others found studios in La Ruche, the counterpart of the Bateau-Lavoir in Montmartre (➤ 158). They were later joined by Russian political refugees, musicians and, between the wars, American writers of the "lost generation", such as Hemingway. They met in cafés along boulevard Montparnasse: La Closerie des Lilas, La Rotonde, Le Select, La Coupole and Le Dôme. Some of their history can be traced in the **Musée du Montparnasse**.

Since the 1960s the district has been modernized. The 200m-high (656ft) **Tour Montparnasse** offers an observation deck, a bar and a restaurant with panoramic views on its 56th floor.

🚇 20T ✉ 75014 🚇 Montparnasse-Bienvenue, Vavin

Musée du Montparnasse

www.museedumontparnasse.net

✚ 20S ✉ 21 avenue du Maine, 75015 ☎ 01 42 22 91 96, 01 42 22 90 16
🕐 Tue–Sun 12:30–7 ✋ Moderate 🚇 Montparnasse-Bienvenue 🚌 28, 48, 58, 89, 91, 92, 94, 95, 96

Tour Montparnasse

www.tourmontparnasse56.com

✚ 20S ✉ Rue de l'Arrivée, 75015 ☎ 01 45 38 52 56 🕐 Apr–Sep daily 9:30–11:30; Oct–Mar Sun–Thu 9:30–10:30; Fri, Sat and the day before a bank holiday 9:30–11 ✋ Expensive 🍴 360 Café (€); Le Ciel de Paris restaurant (€€) 🚇 Montparnasse-Bienvenue 🚌 28, 58, 82, 91, 92, 94, 95, 96 🛈 Gift shop, interactive Paris exhibition at top

ORSAY, MUSÉE D'

Best places to see, ➤ 46–47.

QUAI BRANLY, MUSÉE DU

This popular museum designed by Jean Nouvel and devoted to non-Western cultures stands on pillars above gardens of tall waving grass and exotic plants with the greenery creeping up one of the external walls. The undulating floor of the entry ramp takes you to dimly lit spaces separated by what look like village walls of beaten earth enclosing "music boxes" – multimedia booths that bring the exhibits to life with film and music.

www.quaibranly.fr

✚ 6L ✉ 37 quai Branly/206–218 rue de l'Université, 75007 ☎ 01 56 61 70 00
🕐 Tue–Sun 11–7 (Thu–Sat until 9)
✋ Moderate 🍴 Le Café Branly (€); Restaurant Les Ombres (€€) 🚇 Iéna, Alma-Marceau, École Militaire, Bir-Hakiem; RER Pont de l'Alma 🚌 42, 63, 72, 80, 92 ⛴ Batobus 🛈 Shop

RODIN, MUSÉE

Rodin spent the last few years of his life in the Hôtel Biron as a guest of the French nation; when he died the collection of his works reverted to the State and the mansion was turned into a museum. His forceful and highly original style brought him many disappointments and failures: his *Man with a Broken Nose* (now in the museum) was refused at the 1865 Salon and Rodin had to wait for another 10 years before his talent was fully acknowledged. His major works are inside the museum *(The Kiss, Man Walking)* and in the gardens *(The Thinker, The Burghers of Calais, The Gates of Hell)*.

www.musee-rodin.fr

➕ 19P ✉ 79 rue de Varenne, 75007 ☎ 01 44 18 61 10 🕐 Tue–Sun 9:30–4:45 (5:45 Apr–Sep, park 6:45). Closed 1 Jan, 25 Dec ✋ Moderate 🍴 Cafeteria (€) 🚇 Varenne, Invalides 🚌 69, 82, 87, 92 ❓ Guided tours, shops

ST-GERMAIN-DES-PRÉS

The Benedictine Abbey of St-Germain-des-Prés, founded in the sixth century, was in the Middle Ages so powerful a religious and cultural centre that it became a town within the town. It was completely destroyed during the Revolution; only the church was spared. In spite of many alterations, the church is a fine example of Romanesque style: the tower dates from the 11th century as does the nave; note that the carved capitals on the pillars are copies of the originals kept in the Musée National du Moyen-Âge (➤ 90). You will find vestiges of 13th-century frescoes in the chapel dedicated to St Symphorien. Look in the garden to the left of the entrance for a charming head of the poet Apollinaire by Picasso.

The area between boulevard St-Germain and the river and between rue du Bac and rue de Seine is full of antique shops and art galleries.

www.eglise-sgp.org

➕ 22P ✉ 3 place St-Germain-des-Prés, 75006 ☎ 01 55 42 81 33 🕐 Mon–Sat 8–7:45, Sun 9–8 ✋ Free 🍴 Cafés/restaurants nearby (€–€€) 🚇 St-Germain-des-Prés 🚌 39, 63, 86, 95

ST-SULPICE

The original church, founded by the Abbey of St-Germain-des-Prés, was rebuilt and extended in the 17th century but was not completed until the mid-18th century. The Italian-style facade, by Servandoni, has two slightly different towers. The north tower has recently been restored. Inside are several statues by Bouchardon and outstanding murals by Delacroix (first chapel on the right) as well as a splendid organ by Cavaillé-Coll, traditionally played by the best organists in France. Look on the left-hand wall for the gnomon, an astronomical device installed in the church in 1743 to determine the exact time of equinoxes. As light passes through one of the church's windows it is projected as a luminous disc crossing a line on the floor at noon. Servandoni also submitted plans for the square in front of the church, but they were abandoned and a fountain designed by Visconti was placed in its centre in 1844.

www.paroisse-saint-sulpice-paris.org

➕ 22Q ✉ Place St-Sulpice, 75006 ☎ 01 46 33 21 78 🕐 Daily 7:30–7:30 ✋ Free 🚇 St-Sulpice 🚌 63, 70, 84, 86, 87, 96

LA TOUR EIFFEL

Best places to see, ➤ 54–55.

HOTELS

Hôtel de l'Abbaye (€€€)
A roaring log fire and a delightful inner garden ensure comfort whatever the season.
✉ 10 rue Cassette, 75006 ☎ 01 45 44 38 11; www.hotel-abbaye.com
🚇 St-Sulpice, Sèvres-Babylone

Hôtel d'Angleterre Saint-Germain-des-Prés (€€–€€€)
See page 78.

Hôtel de Nevers (€)
Simple but charming, this hotel occupies a former convent building. In addition to the usual facilities, there are private roof terraces for top-floor rooms.
✉ 83 rue du Bac, 75007 ☎ 01 45 44 61 30;
www.hoteldeneverssaintgermain.com 🚇 Rue du Bac

Hôtel du Quai Voltaire (€€)
All the rooms enjoy panoramic views of the riverbank *bouquinistes* and of the Louvre and Tuileries Gardens across the Seine. The hotel boasts distinguished guests such as Baudelaire, Oscar Wilde and composer Wagner.
✉ 19 quai Voltaire, 75007 ☎ 01 42 61 50 91; www.quaivoltaire.fr
🚇 Palais-Roya-Musée du Louvre

Hôtel Le Régent (€€)
Air-conditioning and bright well-appointed bedrooms are on offer in this cleverly restored 18th-century town house in popular St-Germain-des-Prés.
✉ 61 rue Dauphine, 75006 ☎ 01 46 34 59 80; www.regent-paris-hotel.com
🚇 Odéon

Hôtel Le Tourville (€€–€€€)
Refined decoration for this modern hotel in the elegant 7th *arrondissement*, close to Les Invalides.
✉ 16 avenue de Tourville, 75007 ☎ 01 47 05 62 62; www.tourville.com
🚇 École Militaire

RESTAURANTS

L'Ami Jean (€–€€)
Chef Stéphane Jégo has made this restaurant the rendezvous of gourmets who enjoy his tasty cuisine from southwest France.
✉ 27 rue Malar, 75007 ☎ 01 47 05 86 89; www.amijean.eu ⏱ Lunch, dinner Tue–Sat; closed Aug ⊕ Invalides

Bistrot du 7e (€)
Attractive bistro near les Invalides, excellent value for money.
✉ 56 boulevard de la Tour-Maubourg, 75007 ☎ 01 45 51 93 08 ⏱ Lunch, dinner; closed Sat and Sun lunch ⊕ Invalides, La Tour Maubourg

Les Bouquinistes (€€)
Fashionable restaurant along the embankment; up-and-coming young chef Guy Savoy has made nouvelle cuisine into an art.
✉ 53 quai des Grands-Augustins, 75006 ☎ 01 43 25 45 94; www.lesbouquinistes.com ⏱ Lunch, dinner; closed Sat lunch and Sun ⊕ Saint-Michel

Brasserie Lipp (€€)
See page 62.

Brasserie Lutetia (€€)
On the ground floor of an art deco hotel, this typical brasserie has been updated by Sonia Rykiel and specializes in regional dishes.
✉ 23 rue de Sèvres, 75006 ☎ 01 49 54 46 76; www.lutetia-paris.com ⏱ Daily 12–11 ⊕ Sèvres-Babylone

Le Ciel de Paris (€€–€€€)
On the 56th floor of the Tour Montparnasse; live music from 9pm.
✉ Tour Montparnasse, 33 avenue du Maine, 75015 ☎ 01 40 64 77 64; www.cieldeparis.com ⏱ Lunch, dinner ⊕ Montparnasse-Bienvenüe

D'Chez Eux (€€)
Bistro specializing in *cassoulet* (bean stew with Toulouse sausage).
✉ 2 avenue Lowendal, 75007 ☎ 01 47 05 52 55; www.chezeux.com ⏱ Lunch, dinner; closed first 3 weeks of Aug ⊕ Ecole Militaire

La Coupole (€€)
See page 62.

Le Divellec (€€€)
See page 62.

Le Dôme (€€–€€€)
Brasserie specializing in all types of seafood established in 1898, and later popular with American writers and painters, including Hemingway. Especially good is the *bouillabaisse*.

✉ 108 boulevard du Montparnasse, 75014 ☎ 01 43 35 25 81 🕐 Lunch, dinner 🚇 Vavin

La Ferrandaise (€€)
The inspired, good-value classic cuisine and the original decoration account for the popularity of this convivial bistro.

✉ 8 rue de Vaugirard, 75006 ☎ 01 43 26 36 36; www.laferrandaise.com 🕐 Mon–Fri lunch, dinner; Sat dinner only 🚇 Odéon

La Frégate (€–€€)
Next to the Musée d'Orsay; good-value traditional French cuisine.

✉ 1 rue de Bac, 75007 ☎ 01 42 61 23 77; www.lafregateparis.com 🕐 Daily 7am–1am 🚇 Rue de Bac, Tuileries

Le Petit Zinc (€)
Despite its name, alluding to the traditional countertop of the little Parisian corner bar, this century-old brasserie is an elegant affair, with an oyster bar, art nouveau tiled walls, and a terrace.

✉ 11 rue St-Benoit, 75006 ☎ 01 42 86 61 00, www.petit-zinc.com 🕐 Daily 12–12 🚇 St-Germain-des-Prés

Le Polidor (€)
Established in 1845, a traditional restaurant serving classic French dishes such as *petit salé aux lentilles*, *bavette à l'échalotte* and *escargots*.

✉ 41 rue Monsieur-le-Prince, 75006 ☎ 01 43 26 95 34; www.polidor.com 🕐 Lunch, dinner

Le Procope (€–€€)
The oldest café in Paris, established in 1686 and known to Voltaire and Benjamin Franklin, now a historic monument.
✉ 13 rue de l'Ancienne Comédie, 75006 ☎ 01 40 46 79 00; www.procope.com ⏱ Daily 10:30am–1am Ⓜ Odéon

La Régalade (€–€€)
Haute cuisine at relatively low prices in an unassuming setting; book well in advance.
✉ 49 avenue Jean Moulin, 75014 ☎ 01 45 45 68 58 ⏱ Lunch, dinner; closed Sat, Sun and Mon lunch Ⓜ Alésia

Thoumieux (€–€€)
High-class brasserie specializing in home-made duck *cassoulet*.
✉ 79 rue Saint-Dominique, 75007 ☎ 01 47 05 49 75; www.thoumieux.com ⏱ Lunch, dinner Ⓜ Invalides

SHOPPING

ANTIQUES
Village Suisse
Very expensive antiques displayed in the former Swiss pavilions of the 1900 World Exhibition.
✉ 78 avenue de Suffren, 54 avenue de la Motte-Picquet, 75015; www.villagesuisse.com Ⓜ La Motte Picquet-Grenelle

BOOKS, CDs AND DVDs
Tea & Tattered Pages
This tiny shop, with its cosy tea room at the back, offers a wide choice of books in English.
✉ 24 rue Mayet, 75006 ☎ 01 40 65 94 35; www.teaandtatteredpages.com Ⓜ Duroc

CHILDREN'S SHOPS
Chantelivre
Specialist bookshop dealing with the subjects that interest kids.
✉ 13 rue de Sèvres, 75006 ☎ 01 45 48 87 90; www.chantelivre.fr Ⓜ Sèvres-Babylone

La Maison des Bonbons
Delicious sweets in all shapes and sizes to tempt those with a sweet tooth.
✉ 14 rue Mouton Duvernet 75014 ☎ 01 45 41 25 55;
www.lamaisondesbonbons.com 🚇 Mouton-Duvernet

DEPARTMENT STORE
Bon Marché Rive Gauche
See page 80.

FASHION
Comptoir des Cotonniers
Classic shirts and skirts for mothers and daughters – timeless casual French elegance.
✉ 11 rue du Commerce, 75015 ☎ 01 45 75 10 29;
www.comptoirdescotonniers.com 🚇 Commerce

Petit Bateau
What all the best-dressed French babies and tots wear. Now stocks clothes for mothers, too.
✉ 26 rue Vavin, 75015 ☎ 0155 42 02 53; www.petit-bateau.com 🚇 Vavin

Sonia Rykiel
The grande dame of French fashion, still making ever-wearable clothes.
✉ 175 boulevard Saint-Germain, 75006 ☎ 01 49 54 60 60;
www.soniarykiel.com 🚇 St-Germain-des-Prés, Rue du Bac

FOOD AND WINES
Boulangerie Poîlane
See page 80.

La Grande Épicerie de Paris
This huge grocery store with its marvellous array of goods is every gourmet's dreamland!
✉ 38 rue de Sèvres, 75007 ☎ 01 44 39 81 00; www.lagrandeepicerie.fr
🚇 Sèvres-Babylone

SHOPPING CENTRES
Marché Saint-Germain
See page 81.

ENTERTAINMENT

BARS AND CLUBS
Cubana Café
A little bit of Havana in the heart of Paris – with posters, pictures
and slogans, cigars and cocktails.
✉ 45 rue Vavin, 75006 ☎ 01 40 46 80 81; www.cubanacafe.com 🚇 Vavin

Le Petit Journal Montparnasse
Le Petit Journal Montparnasse welcomes blues, Latin American,
soul and rock bands as well as jazz.
✉ 13 rue du Commandant-Mouchottes, 75014 ☎ 01 43 21 56 70;
www.petitjournalmontparnasse.com 🕐 Mon–Sat 7am–2am
🚇 Montparnasse-Bienvenüe

Wagg
Fashionable Left-Bank venue offering house, disco and salsa.
✉ 62 rue Mazarine, 75006 ☎ 01 55 42 22 01; www.wagg.fr 🕐 Fri, Sat, Sun
🚇 Odéon

CINEMA
La Pagode
La Pagode is wonderfully exotic, with its painted screens and
Japanese garden. Shows cult classics and recent arty releases in
the original language.
✉ 57 bis rue de Babylone, 75007 ☎ 01 45 55 48 48;
www.etoilecinema.com/location/pagode 🚇 St-François-Xavier

THEATRE, DANCE AND OPERA
Odéon, Théâtre de l'Europe
This venue stages classical and contemporary theatre from all over
Europe, often in languages other than French.
✉ Place de l'Odéon, 75006 ☎ 01 44 85 40 40; www.theatre-odeon.fr
🚇 Odéon

ST-HONORÉ

CHAILLOT

Jardin des Tuileries

The Louvre to the Arc de Triomphe

The area of western Paris, from the Louvre to the Arc de Triomphe is noted more for its grandeur than its charm. It's full of elegant squares, formal gardens, fashionable shops and luxury hotels.

Without a doubt, the greatest attraction is the Musée du Louvre. Northwest lie the Jardin des Tuileries, place de la Concorde and the Champs-Élysées, which leads to the Arc de Triomphe and on to La Défense. South of the Arc de Triomphe you will find the Palais de Chaillot, while north of the Louvre are two of Paris's best shopping streets – rue de Rivoli and rue St-Honoré.

ARC DE TRIOMPHE
Best places to see, ➤ 36–37.

LES CHAMPS-ELYSÉES
Best places to see, ➤ 40–41.

ÉGLISE DE LA MADELEINE

Neoclassical Corinthian columns announce a church that was 85 years in the building: the foundations were laid in 1763, the church was consecrated in 1843. Dedicated by order of Napoleon on the battlefield to the glory of the French army, it is now the parish church of the high-class 8th *arrondissement*. The interior also features sculptures by Rude and Pradier, and two organs made by Aristide Cavaillé-Coll. The organists here have included the composers Camille Saint-Saëns and Gabriel Fauré.

www.eglise-lamadeleine.com

➕ 11J ✉ Place de la Madeleine, 75008 ☎ 01 44 51 69 00 🕐 Daily 9:30–7; public hols variable ✋ Free Ⓜ Madeleine 🚌 24, 42, 52, 84, 94 ❓ Shops, audioguide (inexpensive), occasional evening concerts

FAUBOURG ST-HONORÉ

This "suburb" is centred on the long street of the same name, and is famous for its haute couture establishments as well as for the Palais de l'Élysée, the official residence of the French president.

Leading fashion houses have been established in the area for more than 100 years: some in the rue du Faubourg St-Honoré, others in the avenue Montaigne. Opposite the British Embassy, No 54 opens into a couple of courtyards surrounded by boutiques selling furniture, objets d'art and paintings. Modern art galleries line the avenue Matignon, while the avenue Gabriel, which runs along the Champs-Élysées gardens past the American Embassy, makes for a peaceful stroll.

➕ 9J ✉ 75008 Ⓜ St-Philippe-du-Roule, Madeleine 🚌 52, 83, 93 ❓ A stamp market takes place near the Rond Point des Champs-Élysées on Thu, Sat and Sun 9–6

GRAND PALAIS

Built at the same time as the Pont Alexandre III for the 1900 World Exhibition, this enormous steel-and-glass structure, concealed behind stone walls, is typical of the belle époque style: Ionic columns line the imposing facade and colossal bronze statues decorate the four corners. Restoration works due to finish in 2011 are improving visitor facilities while keeping the building open. Major international art exhibitions are traditionally held in the Galeries Nationales, on the Champs-Élysées side of the building.

The west part of the Grand Palais houses the Palais de la Découverte, inaugurated in 1937 to bring science within the grasp of the general public and keep them informed of the latest scientific developments. There are interactive experiments, documentary films and a planetarium.

www.grandpalais.fr

✚ 9K ✉ Galeries Nationales: 3 avenue du Général Eisenhower, 75008; Palais de la Découverte, avenue Franklin D. Roosevelt, 75008 ☎ Galeries Nationales: 01 44 13 17 17; www.rmn.fr/galeries-nationales-du-grand; Palais de la Découverte: 01 56 43 20 20; www.palais-decouverte.fr
🕐 Galeries Nationales: variable; Palais de la Découverte: Tue–Sat 9:30–6, Sun 10–7 💶 Galeries Nationales: variable; Palais de la Découverte: moderate 🍴 Café-bar (€) Ⓜ Franklin D. Roosevelt, Champs-Élysées-Clemenceau 🚌 28, 42, 52, 72, 73, 80, 83, 93

JARDIN DES TUILERIES

This formal French-style garden was laid out by Le Nôtre in the 17th century. The largest and oldest garden in Paris, it features some trees more than 150 years old. The stately central alleyway stretches from the flower beds near the Arc de Triomphe du Carrousel to the place de la Concorde, where an octagonal ornamental pool is surrounded by statues and flanked by terraces; you will find contemporary art throughout the garden. There is a view of the river and the garden with the Louvre in the background from the Terrasse du Bord de l'Eau running along the riverbank.
www.louvre.fr

✚ 12L ✉ Entrances at place de la Concorde, rue de Rivoli, quai des Tuileries, avenue du Général Lemonnier, passerelle Leopold-Sedar-Senghor
🕐 Daily, from the last Sun of the month to the Sat before the last Sun of the month: Jun–Aug 7am–11pm; Apr–May, Sep 7am–9pm, Oct–Mar 7:30–7:30
💴 Free 🍴 Cafés and ice-cream kiosks (€–€€) 🚇 Tuileries, Concorde, Palais-Royal-Musée du Louvre 🚌 21, 24, 27, 39, 42, 48, 68, 69, 72, 73, 81, 84, 94, 95 and Balabus ❓ Model boats for hire, pony rides, trampolines, playground, bookshop, free guided walks Sat, Sun and public hols in summer, 15:30

JEU DE PAUME

Constructed in the middle of the 19th century, this is one of two pavilions at the entrance of the Jardin des Tuileries. Once the game of *jeu de paume* was superceded by tennis, this building was given over to art, specifically the national collection of Impressionist

paintings. It is now a busy, modern space devoted to photography in all its forms, showing both established and new photographers.
www.jeudepaume.org

🚹 11K ✉ 1 place de la Concorde, 75008 ☎ 01 47 03 12 50 🕐 Wed–Fri 12–7, Sat–Sun 10–7, Tue 12–9 💵 Moderate 🍴 Café (€) 🚇 Concorde
🚌 24, 42, 52, 72, 73, 84, 94 ❓ Shop, cinema

LA GRANDE ARCHE DE LA DÉFENSE

In the modern office enclave of La Défense is a vast square with modern sculptures dominated by the Grande Arche. Inaugurated in 1989 for the bicentenary of the French Revolution, the arch was designed by the Danish architect Otto von Spreckelsen as a perfect hollow cube of glass and white Carrara marble. From the top, 110m (360ft) above ground and accessible by glass lift, a fine view unfolds. At the top you will find a computing museum.
www.grandearche.com

🚹 Off map 5H ✉ 1 parvis de la Défense, 92044 ☎ 01 49 07 27 55
🕐 Apr–Aug daily 10–8, Sep–Mar 10–7 💵 Moderate 🍴 Rooftop Le Ô110 restaurant, daily 10–7 (€–€€), cafés 🚇 La Défense; RER A La Défense 🚌 73, Balabus (Apr–Sep) 🚋 🚹 ❓ Shops, Les Quatre Temps shopping centre

LE LOUVRE

Best places to see, ➤ 44–45.

MUSÉE D'ART MODERNE DE LA VILLE DE PARIS

The east wing of the Palais de Tokyo building is home to 9,000 artworks. In its large, white spaces are Fauves, Dadaists and Surrealists, the School of Paris and modern masters of the early 20th century such as Braque, Brassaï, Breton, Modigliani, Picasso, Utrillo and Arp. Matisse's 1933 *La danse de Paris* is a highlight.
www.mam.paris.fr

🚹 6L ✉ 11 avenue du Président Wilson, 75116 ☎ 01 53 67 40 00
🕐 Tue–Sun 10–6, Thu until 10pm 💵 Free 🍴 Cafe (€) 🚇 Iéna, Alma-Marceau 🚌 32, 63, 72, 80, 92

MUSÉE DES ARTS DÉCORATIFS

The Museum of Decorative Arts is dedicated to Man's ceaseless attempt to combine beauty with functionality. The chronological displays span almost a thousand years from the Middle Ages through the triumph of Classicism to the 21st century. Twice-yearly exhibitions display the fashion and textile collections.

www.lesartsdecoratifs.fr

✚ 13L ✉ 107 rue de Rivoli, 75001 ☎ 01 44 55 57 50 🕔 Tue–Fri 11–6 (Thu until 9pm), Sat–Sun 10–6 👖 Moderate 🍴 Le Saut du Loup restaurant has a café terrace with a fine view of the Eiffel Tower (€) 🚇 Palais-Royal, Tuileries, Pyramides 🚌 1, 27, 39, 48, 68, 72, 81, 95 ❓ Audioguide (free)

MUSÉE CERNUSCHI

In a lovely setting on the edge of Parc Monceau, the mansion of banker and art collector Henri Cernuschi houses his superb collection of ancient Chinese art (terracottas, bronzes, jades and ceramics) and contemporary traditional Chinese paintings.

www.cernuschi.paris.fr

✚ 9G ✉ 7 avenue Vélasquez, 75008 ☎ 01 53 96 21 50 🕔 Tue–Sun 10–6; closed public hols 👖 Free 🚇 Villiers, Monceau 🚌 30, 94

MUSÉE JACQUEMART-ANDRÉ

This elegant 19th-century mansion houses the collections of European art bequeathed by a wealthy widow to the Institut de France. French 18th-century art includes paintings by Boucher, Chardin, Greuze and Watteau, as well as sculptures by Houdon and Pigalle, furniture, Beauvais tapestries and objets d'art. There are also 17th-century Dutch and Flemish masterpieces and Italian Renaissance art including works by Donatello and Botticelli.

www.musee-jacquemart-andre.com

➕ 9H ✉ 158 boulevard Haussmann, 75008 ☎ 01 45 62 11 59 🕐 Daily 10–6; temporary exhibitions Mon until 9:30 ✋ Moderate 🍴 Tea room (€) Ⓜ Miromesnil, St-Philippe-du-Roule 🚌 22, 28, 43, 52, 54, 80, 83, 84, 93 ❓ Audioguide (free)

MUSÉE MARMOTTAN-MONET

The museum was named after Paul Marmottan, who bequeathed his house and his private collections of Renaissance and 18th- and 19th-century art to the Institut de France. These were later enriched by several bequests, including 100 paintings by Monet donated by his son: detailed studies of Monet's garden in Giverny, paintings of Rouen Cathedral (executed in different light conditions according to the time of day) and of the River Thames in London. Most important of all, perhaps, *Impression, Soleil levant* (1872), which gave its name to the Impressionist movement. There are also works by Monet's contemporaries, Renoir, Pissarro, Sisley and Gauguin. The basement houses temporary exhibitions.

www.marmottan.com

➕ Off map 5L ✉ 2 rue Louis Boilly, 75016 ☎ 01 44 96 50 33 🕐 Wed–Sun 11–6, Tue 11–9. Closed 1 Jan, 1 May, 25 Dec ✋ Moderate 🍴 Cafés and restaurants (€–€€) in nearby place de la Muette Ⓜ La Muette 🚌 22, 32, 52, 63 ❓ Shops

MUSÉE NATIONAL DES ARTS ASIATIQUES-GUIMET

This museum's collections, spanning 5,000 years, illustrate all the major civilizations of the Asian continent, with special emphasis on calligraphy, painting, gold plate and textiles. Included in the price of entry is the Buddhist pantheon Panthéon Bouddhique at 19 avenue d'Iéna, turn left as you exit the main museum.

www.guimet.fr

➕ 6K ✉ 6 place d'Iéna, 75016 ☎ 01 56 52 53 00 🕐 Tue–Sun 10–6 ✋ Moderate 🍴 Café Ⓜ Boissiére, Iéna 🚌 22, 30, 32, 63, 82 ❓ Audioguide (free)

MUSÉE NISSIM DE CAMONDO

This museum offers a delightful journey back in time to the 18th century, for although the mansion dates from the early 20th century it was modelled on the Petit Trianon at Versailles. The interior includes 18th-century panelling, Aubusson tapestries and Savonnerie carpets, paintings by Elisabeth Vigée Lebrun, sculptures by Jean-Antoine Houdon, and Sèvres and Chantilly porcelain. More recent are an enormous traditional bathroom and the grand kitchens and servants' dining hall.

www.lesartsdecoratifs.fr

🚇 9G ✉ 63 rue de Monceau, 75008 ☎ 01 53 89 06 50 🕐 Wed–Sun 10–5:30. Closed 1 Jan, 14 Jul, 25 Dec ♿ Moderate Ⓜ Villiers 🚌 30, 84, 94 ❓ Guided tours

MUSÉE DE L' ORANGERIE

The tastefully renovated Orangerie houses the Walter-Guillaume collection of Impressionist and 20th-century art, with works by Modigliani, Rousseau, Cézanne, Renoir, Matisse and Picasso and frequent temporary exhibitions. However, the highlight is the complete cycle of Monet's *Nymphéas* (Water Lilies), inspired by the artist's garden at Giverny, which Monet himself chose to install here in a specially designed space. The effect is sublime.

www.musee-orangerie.fr

🚇 11L ✉ Jardin des Tuileries, 75001 ☎ 01 44 77 80 07 🕐 Wed–Mon 9–6 ♿ Moderate Ⓜ Concorde 🚌 24, 42, 52, 72, 73, 84, 94 ❓ Guided tours, shops, audioguide (inexpensive)

MUSÉE DU VIN

Here, in the rue des Eaux, in medieval cellars in an area of natural springs *(eaux)*, amid stacked barrels, wine-making equipment and atmosphere, you can learn all about varieties of grape and wine regions. A glass of wine is included in the price of admission. If you wish to taste more, you can repair to the museum's simple restaurant, whose three vaulted cellars formed part of the wine store of Passy monastery in the 16th and 17th centuries. At that time vines were harvested on nearby slopes to make a light red wine favoured by Louis XIII.

www.museeduvinparis.com

➕ Off map 5M ✉ Square Charles Dickens, rue des Eaux, 75016 ☎ 01 45 25 63 26 🕐 Tue–Sun 10–6 ✋ Expensive, free for restaurant diners 🍴 Restaurant Tue–Sun 12–3 🚇 Passy; RER C Champs de Mars-Tour Eiffel 🚌 72 ❓ Audioguide (free), guided tours, wine tasting classes

OPÉRA GARNIER

The neoclassical Palais Garnier (named after its architect) was opened in 1875. Its exuberant decoration includes a group of statues called *La Danse* by Carpeaux; the group is a copy of the original sculptures which are now in the Musée d'Orsay. Inside, the grand staircase and the foyer are magnificent. In the main hall, restored to its original splendour, visitors can now fully appreciate the ceiling decorated by Chagall. The building sits on an underground lake, and was the inspiration for Gaston Leroux's story *Phantom of the Opera*.

The museum contains paintings, watercolours and pastels illustrating the history of opera and ballet from the 18th century to the present day, mainly through portraits.

www.operadeparis.fr

➕ 12J ✉ Place de l'Opéra, 75009 ☎ 08 92 89 90 90; 01 71 25 24 23 🕐 Daily 10–5. Closed 1 Jan, 1 May and matinee performances ✋ Moderate 🚇 Opéra 🚌 20, 21, 22, 27, 29, 42, 52, 53, 56, 66, 68, 81, 95 ❓ Guided tours in English, shops

PALAIS DE CHAILLOT

Designed for the 1937 World Exhibition, the building consists of two separate pavilions with curved wings, on either side of a vast terrace decorated with monumental statues. Just below, the tiered Jardins du Trocadéro extend to the edge of the river.

The building is home to the Cité de l'architecture et du patrimoine, the Musée National de la Marine, the Théâtre National de Chaillot and the Museé de l'Homme. The Cité de l'architecture et du patrimoine will take you on a tour around the architecture of France from medieval times to the present day. The Musée National de la Marine includes French navy vessels, passenger and merchant marine. The Musée de l'Homme examines mankind.
www.lacollinedesmusees.com; **www.**citechaillot.fr

✚ 5L ✉ Place du Trocadéro, 75016 ☎ Cité de l'architecture et du patrimoine: 01 58 51 52 00; Musée de la Marine: 01 53 65 69 69; www.musee-marine.fr; Musée de l'Homme: 01 44 05 72 72; www.museedelhomme.fr 🕐 Cité de l'architecture et du patrimoine: Wed–Mon 11–7 (Thu until 9); closed Tue, 1 Jan, 1 May, 25 Dec. Musée de la Marine: Wed–Mon 10–6; closed Tue, 25 Dec, 1 Jan, 1 May. Musée de l'Homme: closed for refurbishment until 2012 ✋ All three museums: moderate 🍴 Cafés and restaurants 🚇 Trocadéro, Iéna 🚌 22, 30, 32, 63, 72, 82 ⛴ Batobus to Tour Eiffel

PALAIS-ROYAL

The palace built by Richelieu and bequeathed to Louis XIV now houses the Ministry of Culture, but you can visit the gardens – a haven of peace augmented with modern art. An 18th-century addition houses the Comédie-Française, France's national theatre.
www.monuments-nationaux.fr

✚ 13L ✉ Jardin du Palais-Royal, 6 rue de Montpensier, 75001 ☎ 01 42 96 13 32 🕐 Jun–Aug daily 7am–11pm; Apr–May 7am–10:15pm; Sep

7am–9:30pm; Oct–Mar 7:30am–8:30pm 🖐 Free 🍴 Cafés and restaurants
(€–€€€) 🚇 Palais-Royal-Musée du Louvre 🚌 21, 27, 39, 48, 69, 72, 81, 95

PALAIS DE TOKYO
This exhibition space shows the very latest in contemporary art in
an interior deconstructed to serve as an edgy concrete bunker. The
café is popular with a buzzy crowd, while skateboarders hang out
on the terrace which offers a stunning view of the Eiffel Tower.
www.palaisdetokyo.com
➕ 6L ✉ 13 avenue du Président Wilson, 75016 ☎ 01 47 23 54 01
🕐 Tue–Sun 12–12. Closed 1 Jan, 1 May, 25 Dec 🖐 Moderate 🍴 Café (€)
🚇 Iéna, Alma-Marceau; RER C Pont d'Iéna 🚌 32, 42, 63, 72, 80, 82, 92

PETIT PALAIS
The Petit Palais displays some real treasures – among them 16th-
century Russian icons, art nouveau glass, Roman bronzes, the
plans of the Champs-Élysées, furniture and jewellery by Guimard
(the creator of the emblematic entrances to the Paris métro),
paintings by Gustave Doré, Renoir, Sisley, Monet, Pissaro,
Cézanne and Gaugin. The building has sweeping wrought-iron
banisters, marble pillars, mosaic floors and fresco'd ceilings.
www.petitpalais.paris.fr
➕ 9K ✉ Avenue Winston Churchill, 75008 ☎ 01 53 43 40 00 🕐 Tue–Sun
10–6 (Thu until 8 for temporary exhibitions only) 🖐 Free 🍴 Garden café (€)
🚇 Champs-Élysées-Clemenceau, Concorde 🚌 42, 72, 73, 80, 93
❓ Bookshop, audioguide (inexpensive)

PINACOTHEQUE
The privately owned Pinacothèque specializes in exhibitions of
contemporary art. Advance booking is recommended.
www.pinacotheque.com
➕ 11J ✉ 28 place de la Madeleine, 75008 ☎ 01 42 68 02 01 🕐 Daily
10:30–6 (Wed until 9pm) 🖐 Varies according to exhibition, usually moderate
🚇 Madeleine 🚌 24, 42, 52, 84, 94

PLACE DE LA CONCORDE

This is undoubtedly the most impressive square in Paris: its stately elegance, its size and its magnificent views are simply breathtaking. Built in the mid-18th century, it was designed by Gabriel who erected two Classical pavilions on either side of the rue Royale; its octagonal shape is emphasized by eight allegorical statues representing major French cities.

The pink granite obelisk from Luxor, offered to the French nation by the viceroy of Egypt and erected at the centre of the square in 1836. It is flanked by two graceful fountains. Two magnificent vistas open up: west to the Champs-Elysées and east to Le Louvre beyond the beautiful gates of the Jardin des Tuileries; north towards the Madeleine at the end of the rue Royale and south to the Assemblée Nationale across the pont de la Concorde.

➕ 11K ✉ 75008 🚇 Concorde 🚌 24, 42, 52, 72, 73, 84, 94

PLACE VENDÔME

This square illustrates Louis XIV's style at its best, Classical and elegant without being too emphatic. It was designed by Jules Hardouin-Mansart at the end of the 17th century and an equestrian statue of the King was placed in its centre. However, the statue was destroyed during the Revolution and in 1810 Napoleon had a tall bronze-clad column erected in its place, to commemorate the battle of Austerlitz. Today Paris's top jewellers are based here.

➕ 12K ✉ 75001 🚇 Madeleine, Opéra 🚌 42, 52, 72

PONT ALEXANDRE III

This is Paris's most ornate bridge, named after the Tsar of Russia to celebrate the Franco-Russian alliance. Its sole arch spanning the Seine is in line with the Invalides on the Left Bank while, on the Right Bank, the avenue Winston Churchill leads straight to the Champs-Elysées. The bridge is decorated with exuberant allegorical sculptures surmounted by gilt horses.

➕ 9L ✉ Cours La Reine/Quai d'Orsay 🚇 Invalides 🚌 63, 72, 83, 93

HOTELS

Four Seasons George V (€€€)
See page 78.

Hôtel Astrid (€€)
No two bedrooms are the same in the Astrid, which lies close to the Champs-Élysées. Styles include country and romantic.
✉ 27 avenue Carnot, 75017 ☎ 01 44 09 26 00; www.hotel-astrid.com
🚇 Charles de Gaulle-Étoile

Hôtel Galileo (€€)
This modern hotel has well-appointed rooms; a few have verandas.
✉ 54 rue Galilée, 75008 ☎ 01 47 20 66 06; www.galileo-paris-hotel.com
🚇 George V

Hôtel Hameau de Passy (€€)
A simple, recently renovated hotel, in a leafy courtyard in elegant Passy. Each set of rooms has its own staircase and elevator.
✉ 48 rue de Passy, 75016 ☎ 01 42 88 47 55; www.paris-hotel-hameaudepassy.com 🚇 Passy, La Muette

Hôtel Louvre Marsollier Opéra (€€)
In 1899, Oscar Wilde lived here for a while. The place has retained its old-world charm while offering all the latest facilities.
✉ 13 rue Marsollier, 75002 ☎ 01 42 96 68 14;
www.hotellouvremarsollier.com 🚇 Pyramides, Quatre Septembre

Hôtel Meurice (€€€)
See page 78.

Hôtel Relais du Louvre (€€)
Warm colours, antique furniture and modern comfort.
✉ 19 rue des Prêtres-Saint-Germain-l'Auxerrois, 75001 ☎ 01 40 41 96 42;
www.relaisdulouvre.com 🚇 Louvre-Rivoli

Hôtel Ritz Paris (€€€)
See page 79.

RESTAURANTS

Bon (€€)
Trendy restaurant decorated by Philippe Starck; some vegetarian dishes on the Asian-themed menu.

✉ 25 rue de la Pompe, 75016 ☎ 01 40 72 70 00; www.restaurantbon.fr
🕐 Lunch, dinner 🚇 La Muette

Café le Jardin du Petit Palais (€)
Simple café in the elegant surroundings of the Petit Palais.

✉ Avenue Winston Churchill, 75008 ☎ 01 40 07 11 41 🕐 Tue–Sun 10–5
🚇 Champs-Élysées-Clemenceau

La Cantine du Faubourg (€€)
New establishment with a menu featuring many Asian dishes.

✉ 105 rue du Faubourg-Saint-Honoré, 75008 ☎ 01 42 56 22 22;
www.lacantine.com 🕐 Mon–Fri 11am–4am, Sat–Sun 7pm–4am 🚇 Saint Phillipe-du-Roule, Miromesnil

Chez Clément Élysées (€)
Home-style cooking in charming surroundings, with a glass roof.

✉ 123 avenue des Champs-Élysées, 75008 ☎ 01 40 73 87 00 🕐 Noon–1am
🚇 Charles de Gaulle-Étoile

Cristal Room, Maison Baccarat (€€–€€€)
In a fairytale mansion and designed by Philippe Starck, this is an ideal setting for the seasonal updated French classics.

✉ 11 place des Etats-Unis, 75116 ☎ 01 40 22 11 10; www.baccarat.com
🕐 Lunch, dinner; closed Sun 🚇 Boissière, Kléber, Iéna

Dominique Bouchet (€€)
Refined haute cuisine offered by a renowned French chef.

✉ 11 rue Treilhard, 75008 ☎ 01 45 61 09 46; www.dominique-bouchet.com
🕐 Lunch, dinner; closed Sat–Sun and 3 weeks in Aug 🚇 Miromesnil, Saint-Augustin

Grand Véfour (€€€)
See page 63.

La Maison d'Alsace (€€)
Alsatian specialities and seafood; there is a terrace for warm days.
✉ 39 avenue des Champs-Elysées, 75008 ☎ 01 53 93 97 00;
www.restaurantalsace.com 🕐 24 hours 🚇 Franklin D. Roosevelt

Pierre Gagnaire (€€€)
See page 63.

Timgad (€€€)
See page 63.

SHOPPING

ANTIQUES
Louvre des Antiquaires
A historic building housing about 250 high-class antique dealers.
✉ 2 place du Palais Royal, 75001 ☎ 01 42 97 27 27; www.louvre-
antiquaires.com 🕐 Tue–Sun 11–7; closed Sun in Aug 🚇 Palais Royal-Musée
du Louvre 🚌 21, 24, 27, 67, 69, 72, 74, 81, 95

DEPARTMENT STORES
Au Printemps
See page 80.

Galeries Lafayette
See page 81.

FASHION – BOUTIQUES AND ACCESSORIES
Hermès
Silk scarves and luxury leather goods from this historic, now high-
fashion house.
✉ 24 rue du Faubourg Saint-Honoré, 75008 ☎ 01 40 17 47 17;
http://france.hermes.com 🚇 Concorde

Walter Steiger
Luxury shoes for men and women.
✉ 83 rue du Faubourg Saint-Honoré, 75008 ☎ 01 42 66 65 08;
www.waltersteiger.com 🚇 Miromesnil

FOOD AND WINES

Les Caves Augé

Established in 1850, the oldest wine shop in Paris holds tastings.

✉ 116 boulevard Haussmann, 75008 ☎ 01 45 22 16 97;
www.cavesauge.com 🕓 Closed one week in Aug 🚇 Saint-Augustin

Dubois et Fils

Sells an amazing range of cheese and supplies top restaurants.

✉ 80 rue de Tocqueville, 75017 ☎ 01 42 27 11 38 🚇 Malesherbes, Villiers

Fauchon and Hédiard

See page 80.

Ladurée

This shop and its teashop is the high temple of macaroons.

✉ 16 rue Royale, 75008 and branches ☎ 01 42 60 21 79; www.laduree.com
🕓 Daily 8:30–7:30 🚇 Concorde, Madeleine

Lenôtre

Succulent cakes that melt in the mouth!

✉ 15 boulevard de Courcelles, 75008 ☎ 01 45 63 87 63; www.lenotre.fr
🚇 Villiers

Maille

Dijon mustard in gift boxes and mustard jars in Provencale faience.

✉ 6 place de la Madeleine, 75008 ☎ 01 40 15 06 00 🚇 Madeleine

MISCELLANEOUS GIFTS

Bernardaud

Porcelain, jewellery, original gifts and quality brand names.

✉ 11 rue Royale, 75008 ☎ 01 47 42 82 66; www.bernardaud.fr
🚇 Concorde, Madeleine

La Maison du Chocolat

Want to try the best chocolate in Paris?

✉ 225 rue du Faubourg Saint-Honoré, 75008 ☎ 01 42 27 39 44;
www.lamaisonduchocolat.com 🚇 Ternes

Pylones
Useful gifts, from corkscrews to shopping trolleys, made fun.
✉ 23 boulevard de la Madeleine, 75001 ☎ 01 42 61 08 26,
www.pylones.com 🚇 Madeleine

SHOPPING CENTRES
Carrousel du Louvre
Elegant shopping centre with bars and cafés.
✉ 99 rue de Rivoli, 75001 ☎ 01 43 16 47 10, www.carrouseldulouvre.com
🚇 Palais-Royal

Drugstore Publicis
A futuristic frontage hides a mall with restaurants and gift shops.
✉ 133 avenue des Champs-Elysées, 75008 ☎ 01 44 43 79 00;
www.publicisdrugstore.com 🚇 Charles de Gaulle-Étoile

TOY SHOP
Au Nain Bleu
The most famous toy shop in Paris sells tailor-made teddy bears.
✉ 5 boulevard Malesherbes, 75008 ☎ 01 42 65 20 00;
http://boutique.aunainbleu.com 🚇 Madeleine

ENTERTAINMENT
CABARET AND MUSIC HALL
Crazy Horse Saloon
One of the best glamour shows in Paris with striking colours.
✉ 12 avenue George V, 75008 ☎ 01 47 23 32 32;
www.lecrazyhorseparis.com 🚇 Alma-Marceau, George V

Le Grand Rex
This art deco masterpiece, the biggest and oldest surviving
cinema in Paris, offers a behind-the-screens tour.
✉ 1 boulevard Poissonière, 75002 ☎ 01 45 08 93 58; www.legrandrex.com
🕐 Wed–Sun 10–7 🚇 Bonne Nouvelle

Le Lido
See page 72.

L'Olympia
Once the most popular music-hall in France, the renovated
Olympia now hosts concerts and shows.
✉ 28 boulevard des Capucines, 75009 ☎ 01 55 27 10 00;
www.olympiahall.com 🚇 Opéra

CONCERT VENUES
Salle Pleyel
Traditional concert hall and home to the Orchestre de Paris.
✉ 252 rue du Faubourg Saint-Honoré, 75008 ☎ 01 42 56 13 13;
www.sallepleyel.fr 🚇 Ternes, Charles de Gaulle-Étoile

Théâtre des Champs-Élysées
See page 72.

SPORT
Hippodrome d'Auteuil
Steeplechasing; Grand Steeplechase de Paris, May or June.
✉ Route d'Auteil aux Lacs, Bois de Boulogne, 75016 ☎ 01 40 71 47 47;
www.france-galop.com 🚇 Porte d'Auteuil

Hippodrome de Longchamp
Flat-racing; Grand Prix de Paris in late June or July, Prix de l'Arc de
Triomphe in October.
✉ Route des Tribunts, Bois de Boulogne, 75016 ☎ 01 44 30 75 00;
www.france-galop.com 🚇 Porte Maillot and 🚌 244

Roland Garros
Venue every year in late May and early June for the French Open
tennis tournament.
✉ 2 avenue Gordon Bennett, 75016 ☎ 01 47 43 48 00;
www.rolandgarros.com 🚇 Porte d'Auteuil

Stade Jean Bouin
Home of the Stade Français CASG Rugby, a top rugby union team.
✉ 26 avenue du Général Sarrail, 75016 ☎ 01 40 71 71 00; www.stade.fr
🚇 Porte d'Auteuil

Le Marais and Bastille

Originally a marsh on the Right Bank of the Seine, the Marais was drained in the 13th century and cultivated by monks and the Knights Templar. Once the place des Vosges was constructed at the beginning of the 17th century the district became fashionable and much of the beautiful domestic architecture that still gives the Marais its appeal dates from this period. During the 19th century, many of these *hôtels particuliers* (grand mansions) were divided into workshops and homes for the refugee Jewish community until they were deported by the Nazis. The Marais then declined, but in the 1970s it was rediscovered and revived.

To the west is the Beaubourg district, renowned for its ultra-modern Les Halles shopping centre, and the Centre Georges Pompidou, with its world-famous art collections. To the east lies the Bastille district, forever associated with the French Revolution when the dreaded fortress was stormed by the people of Paris on 14 July 1789, and later razed to the ground. Today the area is lively with bars and restaurants, especially popular with the gay community, and is a magnet for Sunday shoppers.

RÉPUBLIQUE

LES HALLES

Cimetière du
Père-Lachaise

LE MARAIS

BASTILLE

BASTILLE

The outline of the 14th-century fortress stormed by the revolutionaries of 1789 is marked on the paving stones of the place de la Bastille. In the centre stands a 50m-high (164ft) column erected in memory of the victims of the 1830 and 1848 Revolutions, who were buried beneath the base and whose names are carved on the shaft. The column is surmounted by the gilt winged figure of the Spirit of Liberty by Dumont.

The **Opéra Bastille** was inaugurated for the bicentenary of the 1789 Revolution. Designed by the Canadian architect Carlos Ott, it is a harmonious building with a curved facade in shades of grey that glitters in the sun and glows at night. The acoustics of the main auditorium, which can accommodate 2,700 spectators, are superb and the stage is sophisticated.

Behind the opera house, along the avenue Daumesnil, is **Viaduc des Arts**, a disused railway viaduct converted at street level into workshops and showrooms, Above these, the Promenade Plantée is a rooftop-level walkway lined with small gardens that extends to the edge of the Bois de Vincennes

✚ 28P

Opéra Bastille

✉ Place de la Bastille, 75012

☎ Recorded information: 01 40 01 19 70; www.operadeparis.fr 🕐 Times vary; listen to the recorded information. Closed Sun

✋ Moderate–expensive 🍴 Bar 🚇 Bastille
🚌 20, 29, 65, 69, 76, 86, 87, 91 ❓ Guided tours only, shops

Viaduc des Arts

✉ 9–129 avenue Daumesnil, 75012

☎ www.viaducdesarts.fr 🕐 Variable; most workshops open Sun 🍴 Nearby (€)
🚇 Bastille, Ledru Rollin, Gare de Lyon
🚌 29

BIBLIOTHÈQUE NATIONALE DE FRANCE: RICHELIEU

Until 1996, the BN, as Parisians call it, was housed in Cardinal Mazarin's former palace situated at the back of the Palais-Royal, extended many times and now stretching from the rue de Richelieu to the rue Vivienne. Then a new library, over the river in the 13th *arrondissement*, was commissioned by President Mitterrand (▶ 86). Now known as Bibliothèque Nationale site Richelieu, the 18th-century Marais building houses manuscripts, maps, photography, prints and medals and also contains treasures such as the throne of Dagobert and the fan of Diane de Poitiers. Temporary exhibitions are held in the Galerie Mansart (Galerie de Photographie), the Galerie Mazarine (which has a magnificent painted ceiling) and the Crypte. The Cabinet des Médailles et des Antiques displays coins and medals from antiquity to the present day as well as objets d'art, cameos and bronzes from the former royal collections. Renovations are planned from 2014 to 2016.

Two attractive arcades linked to the library, the Galerie Vivienne and the Galerie Colbert, offer an unexpected insight into Parisian social life in the 19th century.

www.bnf.fr

✚ 13K ✉ 58 rue de Richelieu, 75002 ☎ 01 53 79 59 59 🕐 Tue–Sat 10–7, Sun 12–7. Closed Mon am, 7–20 Sep and public hols 💷 Moderate 🚇 Bourse, Palais-Royal Pyramides 🚌 20, 29, 39, 67, 74, 85 ❓ Guided tours (inexpensive)

CENTRE GEORGES POMPIDOU

Best places to see, ▶ 38–39.

CIMETIÈRE DU PÈRE-LACHAISE

The rising ground and abundant vegetation give this cemetery a romantic atmosphere even though more than a million people have been buried here since it was opened by Napoléon I, and more than 2 million visit every year. The tombs of the famous include those of Chopin, Molière, Oscar Wilde, Edith Piaf, Balzac, even the unhappy lovers Héloïse and Abélard. One of the most visited graves is that of Jim Morrison, lead singer of The Doors. In the southeast corner stands the Mur des Fédérés where the last "communards" were shot in 1871.

www.pere-lachaise.com

✚ Off map 28P ✉ 8 boulevard de Ménilmontant, 75020 ☎ 01 55 25 82 10
🕐 Mon–Fri 8–6, Sat 8:30–6, Sun 9–6 (5:30 in winter) ✋ Free 🚇 Père-Lachaise
❓ Guided tours (in English) Sat 3pm in summer

GRANDS BOULEVARDS

These busy arteries, stretching from the place de la République to the Madeleine and lined with cinemas, theatres, cafés and shops, have today fallen victim to their success, choked by traffic jams and disfigured by aggressive neon signs, cheap snack bars and general neglect. The "boulevards" were laid out as a tree-lined promenade in the 17th century, when some of the city's medieval fortifications were demolished; two ceremonial arches, the Porte St-Martin and the Porte St-Denis, replaced the town gates.

The popularity of the boulevards peaked during the 19th century, with popular attractions in the east (theatre, dancing, circus and busking) and more refined entertainment in the west, especially after the building of the opera house. Several shopping arcades were also opened, including the Passage des Panoramas in boulevard Montmartre, and at the end of the century, one of the first cinemas was inaugurated in boulevard St-Denis by the Lumière brothers.

Today, the boulevards still attract crowds of cinema- and theatregoers but their shabby appearance also encourages a rowdy element, particularly between the Porte St-Martin and the rue de Richelieu.

✚ 13J ✉ From east to west: boulevards St-Martin, St-Denis, de Bonne Nouvelle, Poissonnière, Montmartre, des Italiens, des Capucines and de la Madeleine Ⓜ République, Strasbourg Saint-Denis, Bonne Nouvelle, Rue Montmartre, Richelieu-Drouot, Opéra, Madeleine

LES HALLES

When the 19th-century steel-and-glass pavilions of Paris's main wholesale food market were removed in 1969, the character of this popular district changed beyond recognition. Between the Église St-Eustache, one of the most beautiful churches in Paris, and a lovely Renaissance fountain a commercial and cultural complex, the Forum des Halles, was built underground surrounded by glass-roofed galleries. Above ground is a garden with a children's area and shaded walks. The underground complex is undergoing renovation, due to finish in 2012.

www.forumdeshalles.com

✚ 15L ✉ Rue Pierre Lescot, rue Rambuteau, rue Berger, 75001 ☎ 01 40 39 03 67 🕐 Forum des Halles: Mon–Sat 10–8 🍽 In the complex (€) 🚇 Les Halles, Châtelet 🚌 21, 29, 38, 47, 58, 67, 69, 70, 72, 74, 75, 76, 81, 85, 96

HÔTEL DE SOUBISE

Rather worn but gradually being restored, this grand rococco mansion shows how the aristocracy of 17th-century France used to live. With the Hôtel de Rôhan (currently closed to visitors) the building forms part of the Musée de l'Histoire de France (Museum of French History). Part of the building is occupied by the National Archives, which mounts temporary exhibitions.

www.archivesnationales.culture.gouv.fr

➕ 26N ✉ 60 rue des Francs-Bourgeois, 75003 ☎ 01 40 27 60 96 🕐 Mon, Tue–Fri 10–12:30, 2–5:30, Sat–Sun 2–5:30 ✋ Inexpensive 🚇 Hôtel de Ville, Rambuteau, Saint-Paul, Châtelet-Les Halles 🚌 29, 58, 67, 69, 70, 72, 74, 75, 76, 96 ❓ Occasional concerts, Sat 5:30

HÔTEL DE SULLY

This newly renovated *hôtel particulier* is one of the finest Louis XIII buildings in Paris, with an orangery and late Renaissance sculpted decorations on the facades. It was bought by Maximilien de Béthune, Duke of Sully, and stayed in the family until the 18th century. Madame de Sévigné and Voltaire both stayed here.

www.monuments-nationaux.fr

➕ 27P ✉ 62 rue Saint-Antoine, 75004 ☎ 01 44 61 21 50 🕐 Daily 9–7 ✋ Free 🚇 Bastille, Saint-Paul 🚌 20, 29, 61, 65, 69, 76, 86, 87, 91 ❓ Bookshop

HÔTEL DE VILLE

The town hall of the city of Paris has been standing on this site since the 14th century. Destroyed by fire during the Paris Commune in 1871, it was rebuilt almost straight away in neo-Renaissance style. Nearby stands the 52m-high (170ft) Tour St-Jacques, recently restored and the only remaining part of a demolished church.

➕ 25P ✉ Place de l'Hôtel de Ville, 75004 ☎ 01 42 75 54 04 🕐 Guided tour by appointment only ✋ Free 🚇 Hôtel de Ville 🚌 38, 47, 58, 67, 69, 70, 72, 74, 75, 76, 96

MAISON EUROPÉENNE DE LA PHOTOGRAPHIE

This centre for photography holds temporary exhibitions, often drawn from the museum's archive which includes images on the printed page and film as well as photographic prints.

www.mep-fr.org

🚹 26P ✉ 5–7 rue de Fourcy, 75004 ☎ 01 44 78 75 00 🕐 Wed–Sun 11–8 ✋ Moderate 🍴 Café 🚇 Saint-Paul, Pont Marie 🚌 67, 69, 76, 96

MUSEÉ D'ART ET D'HISTOIRE DU JUDAÏSME

As well as paintings by Chagall and many rare and beautiful objects from over the centuries, this sumptuous museum also has a collection of fascinating photographs of the Marais a century and more ago when it was the Jewish quarter of Paris. During the Nazi occupation the inhabitants of the Marais were sent to concentration camps and the area has only recently begun to reclaim some of its heritage, with Jewish restaurants and delis opening in the rue des Rosiers.

www.mahj.org

🚹 16L ✉ 71 rue du Temple, 75003 ☎ 01 53 01 86 62 🕐 Mon–Fri 11–6, Sun 10–6. Closed Sat, Rosh Hashana, Yom Kippur, 1 Jan, 1 May ✋ Moderate 🚇 Rambuteau, Hôtel de Ville 🚌 29, 38, 47, 75 ❓ Audioguide (free), library of books and films Mon–Fri 2–6, Sun 10–1, 2–6

MUSÉE DES ARTS ET MÉTIERS

Created in 1794 as a "warehouse for new and useful inventions", this museum in its unlikely home of a renovated abbey is a temple to the great French names of invention and application, such as Foucault, Renault, Blériot and Peugeot. Here you'll find Lavoisier's laboratory, biplanes and old motors as well as the latest in videogames and space-age transport.

www.arts-et-metiers.net

🚹 16 K ✉ 60 rue Réamur, 75003 ☎ 01 53 01 82 00 🕐 Tue–Sun 10–6 (Thu until 9.30) ✋ Moderate 🚇 Arts et Métiers, Réaumur-Sébastopol 🚌 20, 38, 39, 47

MUSÉE CARNAVALET

The Hôtel Carnavalet was the residence of the diarist Madame de Sévigné who depicted Parisian society at the time of Louis XIV. Today, it and the nearby Hôtel Le Peletier de Saint-Fargeau are a splendid museum of the history of the city of Paris from its earliest origins to the present. The extensive collection includes mementoes of Madame de Sévigné, splendid Louis XV and Louis XVI furniture, Marcel Proust's bedroom and the art nouveau reception room of the Café de Paris.

www.carnavalet.paris.fr

✚ 27P ✉ 23 rue de Sévigné, 75003 ☎ 01 44 59 58 58 🕙 Tue–Sun 10–6. Closed some public hols ✋ Free 🍴 Restaurants and cafés nearby in rue des Francs-Bourgeois (€–€€€) 🚇 Chemin Vert, Saint-Paul 🚌 29, 69, 76, 96 ❓ Guided tours, shops

MUSEÉ DE LA CHASSE ET DE LA NATURE

This imaginative museum devoted to hunting and the hunted, spread over two beautifully and wittily restored *hôtels particuliers,* displays not only stuffed birds and tigers, but also fine art featuring animals – both Rubens and Jeff Koons are represented here. See if you can spot the surprise in the hall of mounted heads. Guns and hunting arms from prehistoric to modern times are also on display. As well as the exhibits, it is the playful and intelligent sensibility with which it is organized that makes this a strikingly original establishment.

www.chassenature.org

✚ 26N ✉ 62 rue des Archives, 75003 ☎ 01 53 01 92 40 🕙 Tue–Sun 11–6 ✋ Moderate 🚇 Hôtel de Ville 🚌 29, 75

MUSÉE DE LA CINÉMATHÈQUE

The Cinemathèque's museum celebrates the movies from the silent days to the present, concentrating on technology as much as the resulting footage. Cinema classics run on screens above your head, while all around are magic lanterns, costumes, rare film posters and other treasures from the collection of the great French film historian Henri Langlois, with donations from stars. Evenings see the Café 51 liven up and screenings in the Cinemathèque's auditoriums which draw on its 40,000 films.

The Cinemathèque building, designed by Frank Gehry, is part of a cultural quarter of Paris developing on both sides of the Seine. Across a small park you will find the new Passerelle Simone de Beauvoir, a footbridge that swoops across the Seine to the Bibliothèque Nationale François Mitterrand (➤ 86).

www.cinematheque.fr

✚ Off map 28S ✉ 51 rue de Bercy, 75012 ☎ 01 71 19 33 33 ◉ Mon, Wed–Sat 12–7 (Thu until 10), Sun 10–8. Closed first 3 weeks in Aug ✋ Inexpensive 🍴 Café 51, Wed–Mon 9:30am–10:30pm Ⓜ Bercy 🚌 24, 64, 87 ❓ Audioguide (free), cinema

MUSÉE COGNACQ-JAY

The collections of 18th-century European art bequeathed to the city of Paris by Ernest Cognacq and his wife Louise Jay, founders of the Samaritaine department store (which closed in 2005), are displayed in one of the beautiful mansions of the Marais. The refinement of the Enlightenment period is illustrated by the works of French artists Watteau, Chardin, Fragonard and La Tour, and also by Tiepolo, Guardi and Reynolds. The collection's Rembrandt adds a welcome contrasting note. Various objets d'art, including Saxe and Sèvres porcelain, are also on display.

www.cognacq-jay.paris.fr

✚ 27N ✉ Hôtel de Donon, 8 rue Elzévir, 75003 ☎ 01 40 27 07 21 ◉ Tue–Sun 10–6. Closed public hols ✋ Free 🍴 Nearby (€–€€) Ⓜ Saint-Paul, Chemin Vert, Rambuteau 🚌 29, 69, 76, 96 ❓ Guided tours, bookshop

MUSÉE PICASSO

The Picasso collection was brought together after the artist's death and consists of works donated to the State by his family in lieu of death duties, and his private collection – together totalling more than 200 paintings, sculptures, prints, drawings and ceramics. That the Hôtel Salé, one of the most beautiful mansions in the Marais, was chosen to house this important collection is entirely appropriate, since Picasso himself preferred to live in old buildings. Like many others in the area it had been neglected and was comprehensively yet sensitively restored to turn it into a museum which opened in 1985. Another renovation began in 2010, and the museum will be completely closed to the public over this time. When it reopens in 2012, visitors will again be able to track the different phases of the artist's development, and view the prolific work of one of the most creative minds of the 20th century. The museum is also home to Picasso's own private collection, which includes works by Renoir, Cézanne, Rousseau and Braque.

www.musee-picasso.fr

✚ 27N ✉ Hôtel Salé, 5 rue de Thorigny, 75003 ☎ 01 42 71 25 21
◉ Closed until 2012 Ⓜ Saint-Paul, Saint-Sébastien Froissart, Chemin Vert
🚌 29, 65, 69, 75, 96

PAVILLON DE L'ARSENAL

The late 19th-century iron-and-glass building houses an information centre devoted to Paris's urban planning and architecture throughout its troubled history. The absorbing permanent exhibition "Paris, visite guidée" (Paris, a guided tour) shows the constant evolution of the cityscape by means of a dynamic, chronological display covering the ground, walls and ceiling of the main hall, with models, films and interactive terminals.

www.pavillon-arsenal.com

✚ 27Q ✉ 21 boulevard Morland, 75004 ☎ 01 42 76 33 97 ◉ Tue–Sat 10:30–6:30, Sun 11–7 💲 Free 🍴 Café Ⓜ Sully-Morland, Bastille
🚌 67, 86, 87

PLACE DES VOSGES

This is Paris's oldest square and perhaps the loveliest for its moderate size, its discreet charm, its delightful brick-and-stone architecture and its peaceful central garden. We owe this brilliant piece of town planning to "Good King Henri" (Henri IV) whose

initiative launched the development of Le Marais. The square is lined with identical pavilions over continuous arcading, dormer windows breaking up the monotony of the dark slate roofs; in the centre of the south and north sides stand two higher pavilions, known respectively as the Pavillon du Roi and

Pavillon de la Reine. The square changed names during the Revolution and was finally called "place des Vosges" in 1800 in honour of the first *département* to pay its taxes!

Number 6, where Victor Hugo (1805–85) lived for 16 years, and wrote many of his most important works, such as *Les Misérables*, is now a museum **(Maison de Victor Hugo)**, containing family mementoes, furniture, portraits and some drawings executed by the writer himself.

✚ 27P ✉ 75004 Ⓜ Saint-Paul, Bastille, Chemin Vert 🚌 20, 65, 69, 76

Maison de Victor Hugo

✉ 6 place des Vosges, 75004 ☎ 01 42 72 10 16; www.musee-hugo.paris.fr
🕐 Tue–Sun 10–6. Closed public hols ✋ Free 🍽 Restaurants nearby
(€–€€€) Ⓜ Bastille, Saint-Paul, Chemin Vert 🚌 20, 29, 65, 69, 96

HOTELS

Corail Hôtel (€)

The Corail, located close to the Gare de Lyon métro, RER and train station, is popular with business people. Rooms may lack character but are comfortable.

✉ 23 rue de Lyon, 75012 ☎ 01 43 43 23 54; www.corailparishotel.com

🚇 Gare de Lyon

Hôtel de la Bretonnerie (€€)

This 17th-century mansion in the heart of the Marais combines modern comfort, including internet access, and a tastefully preserved historic setting.

✉ 22 rue Ste-Croix de la Bretonnerie, 75004 ☎ 01 48 87 77 63

🚇 Hôtel de Ville; RER Châtelet-Les Halles

Hôtel Caron de Beaumarchais (€€)

The best of both worlds: an 18th-century town house in the Marais; refined period decoration but with the benefit of air-conditioning in all rooms.

✉ 12 rue Vieille du Temple, 75004 ☎ 01 42 72 34 12; www.carondebeaumarchais.com 🚇 Hôtel de Ville, Saint-Paul

Hôtel Place des Vosges (€)

See page 79.

Hôtel St-Paul Le Marais (€€–€€€)

The St-Paul occupies a former 17th-century convent, close to the Musée Carnavalet. Breakfast is served in a stone-vaulted room.

✉ 8 rue de Sévigné, 75004 ☎ 01 48 04 97 27; www.hotelsaintpaullemarais.com 🚇 Saint-Paul

Hôtel du Vieux Marais (€€)

Though in a venerable building in the heart of the Marais, this hotel's air-conditioned rooms have been updated in a contemporary, streamlined style. Gay-friendly but not exclusively so.

✉ 8 rue du Plâtre, 75004 ☎ 01 42 78 47 22, www.paris-hotel-vieux-marais.com 🚇 Rambuteau

RESTAURANTS

Au Pied de Cochon (€€)
This is a traditional "Les Halles" restaurant; try the pig's trotters and the onion soup.
✉ 6 rue Coquillière, 75001 ☎ 01 40 13 77 00; www.pieddecochon.com
🕐 24 hours 🚇 Les Halles

Bar à Huîtres (€–€€)
Fashionable seafood brasserie, one of a chain of four in Paris. A good place for oyster-lovers.
✉ 33 boulevard Beaumarchais, 75003 ☎ 01 48 87 98 92;
www.lebarahuitres.com 🕐 Lunch, dinner, open until 2am 🚇 Bastille

Breizh Café (€)
No reservations taken at this *crèperie* specializing in authentic Breton *galettes* (buckwheat pancakes) and cider.
✉ 109 rue Veille du Temple, 75003 ☎ 01 42 72 13 77; www.breizhcafe.com
🕐 Wed–Sat 12–11, Sun 12–10 🚇 Filles du Calvaire

Caveau François Villon (€)
An attractive bistro in 15th-century cellars. Live music is played at night. Reservations advisable.
✉ 64 rue de l'Arbre Sec, 75001 ☎ 01 42 36 10 92; www.caveauvillon.com
🕐 Lunch, dinner; closed Mon and Sat lunch, Sun 🚇 Louvre-Rivoli

Chez Jenny (€–€€)
A convivial traditional brasserie offering seafood and Alsatian specialities.
✉ 39 boulevard du Temple, 75003 ☎ 01 44 54 39 00; www.jenny.fr
🕐 Lunch, dinner 🚇 République

Le Dôme du Marais (€–€€)
Imaginative cuisine in a beautiful room based on fresh seasonal produce; historic surroundings.
✉ 53 bis rue des Francs-Bourgeois, 75004 ☎ 01 42 74 54 17;
www.ledomedumarais.fr 🕐 Lunch, dinner; closed Sun, Mon and 3 weeks in Aug 🚇 Hôtel de Ville, Saint-Paul

Le Mont Lozère (€)

A simple traditional bistro opposite the Pompidou Centre, with a well-priced menu full of French favourites, is as popular with local office workers as with hungry art-lovers.

✉ 31 rue Saint Martin, 75003 ☎ 01 48 87 73 00 🕔 Mon–Sat 8am–11pm
🚇 Rambuteau

Le Pamphlet (€€)

Chef Alain Carrère's trendy restaurant where dishes showcase the refined cuisine characteristic of the southwest region of France.

✉ 38 rue Debelleyme, 75003 ☎ 01 42 72 39 24 🕔 Lunch, dinner; closed Sat and Mon lunch, Sun 🚇 Filles du Calvaire, République

Le Pharamond (€–€€)

Traditional food from Normandy, such as Caen-style tripe with cider, served in an historic building with an art nouveau interior.

✉ 24 rue de la Grande Truanderie, 75001 ☎ 01 40 28 45 18; www.pharamond.fr 🕔 Lunch, dinner; closed Sun, Mon 🚇 Les Halles, Etienne Marcel

La Poule au Pot (€€)

A bistro maintaining the culinary traditions connected with Les Halles food market serves dishes from many regions of France.

✉ 9 rue Vauvilliers, 75001 ☎ 01 42 36 32 96; www.lapouleaupot.fr
🕔 Dinner; open until 6am; closed Mon 🚇 Louvre-Rivoli, Les Halles

Terminus Nord (€€)

A 1920s-style brasserie near the Gare du Nord; the speciality is *choucroute*.

✉ 23 rue de Dunkerque, 75010 ☎ 01 42 85 05 15; www.terminusnord.com
🕔 Daily 11am–1am 🚇 Gare du Nord

Vins des Pyrénées (€–€€)

Bustling yet romantic bistro with red-checked tablecloths. Innovative twists on traditional French cuisine.

✉ 25 rue Beautreillis, 74004 ☎ 01 42 72 64 94 🕔 Lunch, dinner until 11:30pm, bar until 2am 🚇 Saint-Paul, Bastille

SHOPPING

ART, ANTIQUES AND HANDICRAFTS
Viaduc des Arts
Former railway viaduct housing beneath its arches workshops
and exhibitions displaying art and handicrafts.

✉ 9–129 avenue Daumesnil, 75012 ☎ www.viaducdesarts.fr Ⓜ Bastille,
Gare de Lyon

Village Saint-Paul
A group of small antiques dealers established between rue St-Paul
and rue Charlemagne.

✉ Le Marais, 75004 ☎ www.village-saint-paul.com Ⓜ Saint-Paul,
Pont Marie

CHILDREN'S SHOPS
Bonton
A veritable department store for chic children, with clothes, toys
and furniture, such as cute lamps.

✉ 5 boulevard des Filles du Calvaire, 75003 ☎ 01 42 72 34 69;
www.bonton.fr Ⓞ Mon–Sat 10–7 Ⓜ Filles du Calvaire

Pain d'Épices
Two floors of traditional toys to delight children, and kits for adults
who want to make toys, in a shop situated in a historic covered
arcade.

✉ 29, 31, 33 Passage Jouffroy 75009 ☎ 01 47 70 08 68;
www.paindepices.fr Ⓞ Mon 12:30–7, Tue–Sat 11–7 Ⓜ Richelieu-Drouout,
Grands Boulevards

FASHION
Agnès B
The epitome of Parisian cool, this label, worn by men, women and
children of all ages, has almost taken over the street, and looks set
to do the same around the rue de Marseille in the stylish 10th
arrondissement.

✉ 2, 3, 6, 19 rue du Jour, 75001 ☎ 01 45 08 56 56; www.agnesb.com
Ⓞ Mon–Sat 10–7 Ⓜ Les Halles

FOOD
Mariage Frères

A byword for elegance, this branch of a small chain stocks the finest flushes of leaf tea beautifully packaged and all the paraphernalia to go with it.

✉ 30 rue du Bourg-Tibourg, 75004 ☎ 01 42 72 28 11; www.mariagefreres.com 🕐 Daily 10:30–7:30 🚇 Saint-Paul, Hôtel de Ville

Murciano

Strudels, home-made biscuits and bread are on sale in a beautiful and venerable kosher bakery that maintains the century-old traditions that have been practised on this once completely Jewish street in the Marais.

✉ 14–16 rue des Rosiers, 75004 ☎ 01 48 87 48 88 🕐 Sun–Thu 8–8, Fri 8–3 🚇 Saint-Paul

PETS
Un Chien Dans le Marais

Little dogs are a popular accessory in Paris, and Parisians love buying little coats and collars for them. Despite its name this shop caters for cats, too.

✉ 35 bis rue du Roi de Sicile, 75004 ☎ 01 42 74 30 06 🕐 Daily 12–7 🚇 Saint-Paul

SHOPPING CENTRE
Forum des Halles

Underground shopping centre on several floors including chain-store fashion boutiques and the new Forum des Créateurs for young designers; also a huge FNAC store.

✉ 101 Porte Berger, 75001 ☎ 01 44 76 96 56; www.forumdeshalles.com 🕐 Mon–Sat 10–8 🚇 Les Halles; RER Châtelet-Les Halles

ENTERTAINMENT

CONCERT VENUE
Théâtre du Châtelet

See page 72.

NIGHTCLUBS AND BARS
Les Bains Douches
Hip rendezvous of models and VIPs, playing varied musical styles.
✉ 7 rue du Bourg-l'Abbé, 75003 ☎ 01 53 01 40 60;
www.lesbainsdouches.net 🚇 Etienne Marcel

La Chapelle des Lombards
Salsa and Afro music; live shows mid-week; smoking room.
✉ 19 rue de Lappe, 75011 ☎ 01 43 57 24 24; www.la-chapelle-des-
lombards.com 🚇 Bastille

Cithéa Nova
Quality live music, disco, jazz, funk, Afro, soul. Stays open until late.
✉ 114 rue Oberkampf, 75011 ☎ 01 40 21 70 95; www.citheanova.com
🚇 Oberkampf

Favela Chic
Fashionable club specializing in Latin American dance and music,
serving food to match.
✉ 18 rue du Faubourg du Temple, 75011 ☎ 01 40 21 38 14;
www.favelachic.com/paris 🚇 République

SPORT
Piscine des Halles
Renovated sports centre with 50m-long (164ft) swimming pool.
✉ Forum des Halles, rue Berger, 75001 ☎ 01 42 36 98 44 🚇 Les Halles

Hippodrome de Vincennes
Trotting races; Prix d'Amérique in late January.
✉ 2 route de la Ferme, 75012 ☎ 01 49 77 14 70; www.hippodrome-
vincennes.com 🚇 Château de Vincennes

Palais Omnisports de Paris Bercy (POPB)
Around 150 international sporting events every year, from athletics
and tennis to show-jumping and basketball. Also hosts concerts.
✉ 8 boulevard de Bercy, 75012 ☎ 01 40 02 60 60; www.bercy.fr
🚇 Bercy, Gare de Lyon

MONTMARTRE

PIGALLE

Montmartre

**This unassuming village overlooking Paris
is best known for the bohemian types who came to live
here in the 19th century, attracted by its picturesque
location and the independent atmosphere.**

La Butte (the hill) Montmartre became a place of recreation for
Parisians in the mid-19th century. They came for music, dancing,
theatre and discussions about politics and literature in the many
cafés and cabarets – one of the first of which was Le Chat Noir. It
was free-thinking, fun and affordable and the artists soon moved
in. Toulouse-Lautrec painted the can-can dancers of the Moulin
Rouge and the myth of Montmartre began.

Today, it is the second most-visited area in Paris and it can be
difficult to find the real character of la Butte among the teeming
tourist traps such as the place du Tertre and the Sacré-Cœur, but
wander off into its narrow, cobbled streets lined with whitewashed
cottages and you may find it lingers here and there.

CIMETIÈRE DE MONTMARTRE

Montmartre's tree-shaded cemetery, which opened its gates in 1825, is one of the most visited in Paris along with Père-Lachaise (➤ 138) and Montparnasse. The tombs that jostle each other here bear famous names such as those of the composers Hector Berlioz (who like many Parisians of his day loved to walk here) and Jacques Offenbach. You will also find the artist Edgar Degas, Adolphe Sax, inventor of the saxophone, the novelist Stendhal, the film director François Truffaut, the great chef Marie-Antoine Carême and the scientist André Ampère. Georges Feydeau, the genius of French farce, and dancers as different as Vaclav Nijinski and the can-can star La Goulue are buried here too.

www.paris.fr

🞉 1C ✉ 20 avenue Rachel, 75018 ☎ 01 53 42 36 30
🕐 16 Mar–5 Nov Mon–Fri 8–6, Sat 8:30–6, Sun 9–6; 6 Nov–15 Mar Mon–Fri 8–5:30, Sat 8:30–5:30, Sun 9–5:30 (last entry 15 min before closing) ✋ Free 🚇 Place de Clichy/Blanche 🚌 Montmartrobus, 30, 54, 74, 80, 95 ❓ Free plan of the graves available at main entrance or download from the City of Paris website www.paris.fr; guided tours available, times vary

ÉGLISE ST-PIERRE

Between the hustle and bustle of the place du Tetre and Sacré-Coeur is one of the oldest churches in Paris, the diminutive Romanesque St-Pierre-de-Montmartre. Consecrated in 1147, this simple, lovely, peaceful church is all that remains of the Benedictine abbey of Montmartre.

🞉 3C ✉ 2 rue du Mont-Cenis, 75018 ☎ 01 46 06 57 63 🕐 Daily 8:45–6 🚇 Abbesses, Anvers, Funicular 🚌 Montmartrobus, 30, 54
❓ Guided visits, 2nd Sun of month, 4pm

ESPACE MONTMARTRE SALVADOR DALÍ

Featuring more than 300 works by the flamboyant artist Salvador
Dalí (1904–89), this collection of sculptures, illustrations,
lithographs and less familiar paintings is the biggest display in
France of the work of the Catalan master of Surrealism.
www.daliparis.com

3C ✉ 11 rue Poulbot, 75018 ☎ 01 42 64 40 10 🕐 Jul–Aug daily 10–8;
Sep–Jun 10–6 🎟 Moderate 🚇 Abbesses, Anvers, then Funicular
🚌 Montmartrobus, 54, 80

MARCHÉ AUX PUCES DE ST-OUEN

Said to be the largest flea market in the world, this sprawls over 7ha (17 acres) just north of Montmartre (➤ 153) and has been on this site for more than a century. More than 2,500 stalls are grouped into 16 different *marchés*, each with its own specialities, from bric-à-brac and second-hand clothes to pricey antiques and wacky 1970s furniture. Be prepared to haggle, pay in cash and keep watch for pickpockets.

www.marchesauxpuces.fr

✚ Off map 4A ✉ Streets around rue des Rosiers, 75018 ⏱ Sat–Mon 9:30–6 (some stalls open earlier) Ⓜ Porte de Clignancourt, Garibaldi 🚌 56, 60, 85, 95

MOULIN DE LA GALETTE

The first windmill was built on the heights of Montmartre in 1570 and there were once 14 on the Butte (hill), but today only two remain, neither of which works. In 1834 the Debray brothers opened the Moulin de la Galette, converting a real 17th-century mill into a dancehall, restaurant and garden, best remembered in Renoir's 1876 painting, *Le Bal du Moulin de la Galette*, now in the Musée d'Orsay (► 46–47). The flour from the mill was originally used to make cakes, biscuits or pancakes named galettes after the flour. Today the building is a restaurant.

✚ 2C ✉ 83 rue Lepic, 75018 ☎ 01 46 06 84 77 🕙 Daily 12–11 for diners only 🍴 Lunch (€), dinner (€€) 🚇 Abbesses 🚌 Montmartrobus, 80

MOULIN-ROUGE

A cabaret venue since 1889, the Moulin-Rouge (Red Windmill) was never actually a windmill. It soon found international fame, however, as the home of the can-can. The local washerwomen who were the first stars of the can-can acquired humorous names such as La Gouloue (the glutton) and La Grille d'Égout (the drain-cover) and were painted by Toulouse-Lautrec. Much more glamorous shows are performed here today, but at a price.
www.moulinrouge.fr

✚ 1D ✉ 82 boulevard de Clichy, 75018 ☎ 01 53 09 82 82 🕙 Daily, dinner and show 7pm, show only 9pm and 11pm ✋ Expensive 🚇 Blanche 🚌 30, 54, 68, 74 ❓ Souvenir shop: 11 rue Lepic, 75018

MUSÉE DE MONTMARTRE

In a house that was once home to the artists Auguste Renoir, Suzanne Valadon and Maurice Utrillo, a variety of exhibits shows the history of the hill village that has always kept itself a little apart from the rest of Paris. As well as many paintings and photographs, you can see a room detailing the bloody history of the commune of 1871 when Montmartre declared its independence from Paris.

Despite such political upheavals, in the second half of the 19th century, rent here was cheap and the atmosphere was easy-going, so the artists soon moved in – a model of the area shows, with flags, where they lived and worked. The celebrated Bateau-Lavoir (now just a reconstructed facade) became artists' studios in 1889 – it was where in 1907 Picasso painted his revolutionary *Les Demoiselles d'Avignon*.

Montmartre's artistic heyday lasted until World War I, when many artists decamped to the Left Bank and Montparnasse.

Here are the originals of the posters that made Montmartre a byword for entertainment in the second half of the 19th century, including Steinlen's for Le Chat Noir cabaret, and Toulouse-Lautrec's of Aristide Bruant, the singer, writer and founder of the Mirliton cabaret. Here, too, you'll see the original signboard for the Lapin Agile (➤ 165) painted by André Gill, and souvenirs and photographs of the early days of the can-can.

www.museedemontmartre.fr

➕ 3C ✉ 12 rue Cortot, 75018 ☎ 01 49 25 89 37 🕐 Tue–Sun 11–6
✋ Inexpensive 🚇 Abbesses, Anvers, Lamarck-Caulaincourt, Funicular
🚌 Montmartrobus, 80 ❓ Bookshop

MUSÉE DE LA VIE ROMANTIQUE

From about 1820, the writers, musicians and artists of the Romantic movement moved into little houses with gardens around Pigalle, which became known as New Athens. This house at the end of a secluded tree-lined lane was home to the painter Ary Scheffer. The composer Frédéric Chopin and his companion, the writer George Sand, were frequent visitors and Franz Liszt was a neighbour. The house is full of paintings and memorabilia, including casts of Chopin's and Sand's hands, and Sand's jewellery, while Chopin's piano music plays in the background. www.vie-romantique.paris.fr

🕂 2E ✉ Hôtel Scheffer-Renan, 16 rue Chaptal, 75009 ☎ 01 55 31 95 67 🕐 Tue–Sun 10–6 (last entry 30 min before closing) 🖐 Free 🍴 Tea in the garden; May–Oct 11:30–5:50; (€) Ⓜ Saint-Georges, Pigalle, Blanche, Liège 🚌 67, 68, 74 ❓ Guided tours

PLACE DU TERTRE

Place du Tertre is filled with easels and would-be artists, all trying to sell their work or sketch you. (You are not obliged to pay if they produce an unsolicited portrait of you.) For most of the year it bustles with crowds who come to eat and people-watch, but during winter it sometimes retains its rural atmosphere. At No 6, on one corner of the square, is La Mère Catherine, an eating place dating from the Napoleonic era. Legend recounts that it was popular with the Russian troops occupying the city in 1814. They would bang the table and shout "bistro!" ("quick!"), so creating the future name for such simple restaurants. Here you can occasionally sample the local wine made in Montmartre.

🕂 3C ✉ Place du Tertre, 75018 🍴 Many restaurants: (€–€€). La Mère Catherine: 6 place du Tertre, tel: 01 46 06 32 69; daily 12pm–12:30am; €€ Ⓜ Abbesses, Funicular 🚌 Montmartrobus

SACRÉ-CŒUR

Best places to see, ➤ 52–53.

LA VILLETTE

Bordered and bisected by attractive waterways, this park is the biggest green space in the city with a dozen special gardens, each planted according to a different theme, red metal "follies" and children's activity areas. In and around the park are the institutions that have made this area a cultural magnet: the **Cité des Sciences et de l'Industrie,** home to science and technology shows, the Cité de la Musique's museum **(Musée de la Musique)** and concert hall, the Grande Halle concert hall, the Théâtre Paris Villette, the Zénith concert hall, the Cabaret Sauvage circus top and the Paris Conservatoire.

Children love to investigate the former naval submarine, the *Argonaute*, while in the Cinaxe the auditorium moves at the same time as the film, and the Géode is a sparkling silver globe which encloses a hemispheric cinema screen. A fashionable crowd makes for the Bassin de la Villette, which is lined with hip hang-outs, including waterside bars and a cinema.

www.villette.com

✚ Off map 4D ✉ Either side of canal de l'Ourcq from avenue Jean Jaurès at Porte de Pantin to avenue Corentin Cariou at Porte de la Villette
☎ 01 40 03 75 75 🕐 24 hours 💶 Free 🚇 Porte de la Villette, Porte de Pantin 🚌 75 🚢 From and to Port de l'Arsenal: Canauxrama (tel: 01 42 39 15 00; www.canauxrama.com); from and to Port de l'Arsenal and Museé d'Orsay: Paris Canal (tel: 01 42 40 96 97; www.pariscanal.com)

Cité des Sciences et de l'Industrie
✉ 30 avenue Corentin-Cariou, 75019 ☎ 01 40 05 80 00; www.cite-sciences.fr 🕐 Tue–Sat 10–6, Sun 10–7 💶 Moderate; exhibitions and planetarium moderate 🍴 Restaurants and cafés (€) 🚇 Porte de la Villette ❓ Children's workshops times vary, booking recommended

Musée de la Musique
✉ Parc et la Grande Halle de la Villette: 211 avenue Jean Jaurès, 75019
☎ 01 44 84 45 00; www.cite-musique.fr 🕐 Tue–Sat 12–6, Sun 10–6
💶 Moderate 🍴 Café de la musique (€) ❓ Concerts daily, audioguides (free; separate children's audioguide), workshops, guided tours and *mediathèque*

HOTELS

Citadines Apart'hotel Montmartre (€€)
This branch of a worldwide chain offering studio or one-bed apartments is well situated at the foot of the Butte, with a fantastic view of Sacré-Coeur from the rooftop terrace (open summer only).
✉ 16 avenue Rachel, 75018 ☎ 01 44 70 45 50; www.citadines.com
🚇 Place de Clichy, Blanche

Hôtel des Arts (€–€€)
Close to Sacré-Cœur and the rue des Abbesses, this comfortable hotel has a warm interior with fine furniture. There is also car parking nearby.
✉ 5 rue de Tholozé, 75018 ☎ 01 46 06 30 52; www.arts-hotel-paris.com
🚇 Abbesses, Blanche

Hôtel Prima Lepic (€€)
The quietest rooms in this tastefully furnished hotel overlook an inner courtyard, while those facing rue Lepic give a fascinating view of bustling Parisian life. Sacré-Cœur and the Moulin-Rouge are both a short walk away.
✉ 29 rue Lepic, 75018 ☎ 01 46 06 44 64; www.hotel-paris-lepic.com
🚇 Blanche/Abbesses

Hôtel Roma Sacré Cœur (€–€€)
This quiet, comfortable hotel is located in the northern residential part of Montmartre, yet within walking distance of the place du Tertre along the picturesque narrow streets that climb the Butte.
✉ 101 rue Caulaincourt, 75018 ☎ 01 42 62 02 02; www.hotelroma.fr
🚇 Lamarck-Caulaincourt

Terrass Hôtel (€€€)
The "terrace" which gives this comfortable, family-run hotel on the lower slopes of the Butte its name is a summer rooftop restaurant which, from May to September, offers a superb view of the Eiffel Tower and the Left Bank.
✉ 12 rue Joseph-de-Maistre, 75018 ☎ 01 46 06 72 85;
www.terrasshotel.com 🚇 Blanche, Abbesses

Tim Hôtel Montmartre (€€)

In the old part of Montmartre, with lovely views; attention to detail makes it a comfortable if simple place to stay.

✉ 11 rue de Ravignan, 75018 ☎ 01 42 55 74 79; www.timhotel.com

🚇 Abbesses, Pigalle

RESTAURANTS

Au Pied du Sacré-Cœur (€)

The cuisine at this restaurant, situated at the foot of Sacré-Cœur, ranges from traditional dishes, such as grilled steak in pepper sauce to more exotic fare, such as poultry stuffed with prawns.

✉ 85 rue Lamarck, 75018 ☎ 01 46 06 15 26; http://aupieddusacrecoeur.free.fr

🕐 Lunch Tue–Sun, dinner daily 🚇 Lamarck-Cauliancourt

Bistrot Poulbot (€€)

This lovely little restaurant offers a menu that changes two or three times a year, and might include a delicious Barbary duck with baby turnips or lamb noisettes with thyme jus.

✉ 39 rue Lamarck, 75018 ☎ 01 46 06 86 00; www.bistropoulbot.com

🕐 Mon–Sat 12:30–2:30, 7:30–10; closed Sun Jun–Sep and 2 weeks in Aug

🚇 Lamarck-Cauliancourt

La Bonne Franquette (€–€€)

Convivial inn-style restaurant rich in mementoes of the artists who used to dine here – Van Gogh, Monet, Cézanne. There is music in the evening, and meals are served in the garden in fair weather.

✉ 2 rue des Saules/18 rue Saint-Rustique, 75018 ☎ 01 42 52 02 42; www.labonnefranquette.com 🕐 Lunch, dinner 🚇 Lamarck-Caulaincourt, Abbesses

Brasserie Wepler (€–€€)

Brasserie Wepler, with its late 19th-century ambience, offers a classic menu that includes an exceptional seafood platter as well as French onion soup, bouillabaisse, duck foie gras, *choucroute*, steak tartare and grilled sirloin. The desserts are outstanding.

✉ 14 place de Clichy, 75018 ☎ 01 45 22 53 24; www.wepler.com

🕐 Daily 8am–1am 🚇 Place de Clichy

Le Chamarré (€€–€€€)
The ambitious modern menu encompasses flavours from France and Mauritius, with fish the speciality. If dinner is beyond your budget, try the much less expensive lunch menu.

✉ 52 rue Lamarck, 75018 ☎ 01 42 55 05 42; www.chamarre-montmartre.com 🕐 Lunch and dinner 🚇 Lamarck-Caulaincourt

Chez Toinette (€)
Chez Toinette is open only for dinner. The beef carpaccio seasoned with ground nutmeg is a popular starter. Then choose from one of the main courses of fish, meat or game. The desserts are exceptional. Credit cards are not accepted; reservations are advisable, especially on Fridays and Saturdays.

✉ 20 rue Germain-Pilon, 75018 ☎ 01 42 54 44 36 🕐 Mon–Sat 7:15pm–11:15pm; closed Aug 🚇 Abbesses

Le Pied à l'Etrier (€)
The traditional French cuisine here is good value for money. Reserve a table in advance.

✉ 154 rue Lamarck, 75018 ☎ 01 42 29 14 01 🕐 Lunch, dinner; closed Mon, Sun and Aug 🚇 Guy Môquet

Le Rendezvous des Chauffeurs (€)
Named after the taxi drivers who ferried French troops to the front in 1914, this unpretentious restaurant, popular with local diners, serves home-style cooking, from juicy steaks with fat *frites* to kidneys, *andouilles* (chitterling sausage) and steak tartare.

✉ 11 rue des Portes-Blanches, 75018 ☎ 01 42 64 04 17 🕐 Thu–Tue noon–2:30, 7–10:30. Closed Aug, Thu in summer 🚇 Marcadet-Poissonniers

Le Virage Lepic (€)
The food in this cosy bistro on one of lower Montmartre's most atmospheric streets, is utterly delicious, and the wine list includes an excellent house champagne. You can sit outside in summer. Reserve in advance.

✉ 61 rue Lepic, 75018 ☎ 01 42 52 46 79 🕐 Wed–Mon 7pm–11pm 🚇 Blanche, Abbesses

SHOPPING

FASHION AND ACCESSORIES
Tati

This enormous branch of Tati (➤ 81) covers several blocks.

✉ 18 boulevard de Rochechouart, 75018 ☎ 01 55 29 50 20; www.tati.fr
🕐 Mon–Sat 10–7 🚇 Barbès-Rochechouart

FOOD AND DRINK
Arnaud Larher

The best cakes in Montmartre, and superb macaroons.

✉ 53 rue Caulaincourt, 75018 ☎ 01 42 57 68 08; www.arnaud-larher.com
🕐 Daily 9–8 🚇 Lamarck-Caulaincourt

Le Marché des Gastronomes

New gourmet food hall and *traiteur*, with regional specialities and wine tastings.

✉ 9 place Piagalle, 75009 ☎ 01 80 06 85 56;
www.lemarchedesgastronomes.com 🕐 Mon–Sat 10–9 🚇 Pigalle

Les Vignes de Montmartre

Advance booking is required for a 45-minute vineyard tour. Fewer than 1,000 bottles of Clos Montmartre are produced each year.

✉ Reservations: Syndicat d'Initiative de Montmartre, 21 place du Tertre,
75018 ☎ 01 42 62 21 21; www.montmartre-guide.com 🚇 Abbesses,
Lamarck-Cauliancourt, Funicular 🚌 Montmartobus

MARKETS
Marché aux Puces de Saint-Ouen

The largest flea market in Paris. Be prepared to bargain (➤ 156).

✉ Streets around rue des Rosiers, 75018 🕐 Sat–Mon 9:30–6 (some stalls
open earlier) 🚇 Porte de Clignancourt, Garibaldi 🚌 56, 60, 85, 95

Marché Saint-Pierre

Huge discount store at the foot of Sacré-Cœur selling high-quality fabrics, tapestries and clothing.

✉ 2 rue Charles Nodier, 75018 ☎ 01 46 06 92 25;
www.marche-saintpierre.fr 🕐 Mon–Sat 10–6:30 🚇 Anvers

MISCELLANEOUS GIFTS
Par amour des textes
For T-shirts, bags and more – decorated with sayings in French.
✉ 22 rue Houdon, 75018 ☎ 01 42 51 20 16; www.paramourdestextes.com
🕐 Tue–Sun 11–8 🚇 Abbesses, Pigalle

ENTERTAINMENT
CABARET
Au Lapin Agile
This venerable Montmartre cabaret makes a great and affordable night out with its mix of popular music and sharp-edged repartee.
✉ 22 rue des Saules, 75018 ☎ 01 46 06 85 87; www.au-lapin-agile.com
🕐 Tue–Sun 9pm–2am 🚇 Lamarck-Caulaincourt

Moulin-Rouge
Undoubtedly the most famous cabaret of them all! The Moulin-Rouge's high-priced show still includes the can-can (▶ 157).
✉ 82 boulevard de Clichy, 75018 ☎ 01 53 09 82 82; www.moulin-rouge.com
🕐 Nightly: 7pm dinner and show; 9pm and 11pm show only 🚇 Blanche

CONCERT VENUES
Le Zénith
This vast concert hall at La Villette hosts big names in pop and rock.
✉ 211 avenue Jean Jaurès, 75019 ☎ 01 40 03 75 75; www.zenith-paris.com
🚇 Porte de Pantin 🚌 75

NIGHTCLUBS
Le Folies Pigalle
The mid-20s crowd grooves to house in a charged atmosphere.
✉ 11 place Pigalle, 75009 ☎ 01 48 78 55 25; www.lefoliespigalle.com
🚇 Pigalle

Le Divan du Monde
A great atmosphere and reasonably priced drinks, with theme nights, with an emphasis on world music.
✉ 75 rue des Martyrs, 75018 ☎ 01 40 05 06 99; www.divandumonde.com
🕐 Tue–Thu 7pm–2am, Fri–Sat 7pm–6am 🚇 Pigalle, Anvers, Abbesses

Excursions

"Île de France", as the Paris region is called, means the heart of France; and this is exactly what it has always been and still is, the very core of the country, a prosperous and dynamic region, inhabited by one-fifth of the French population, with Paris in its centre. Roads, motorways and international railway lines converge on this central region, which has become one of Europe's main crossroads, with two major international airports.

Besides its tremendous vitality, the Île de France offers visitors attractive natural assets, a rich cultural heritage and a gentle way of life. The countryside is domestic rather than spectacular, graced by picturesque villages, country inns, manor houses, historic castles, abbeys, cathedrals and beautiful parks and gardens.

BASILIQUE CATHÉDRALE DE SAINT-DENIS

One of the finest Gothic churches in France, begun in 1145, this is the resting place of the first bishop of Paris, martyred by the Romans *c.*250. In 1805 Napoleon I made Saint-Denis into a royal necropolis, with some 70 tombs.

www.saint-denis.monuments-nationaux.fr

✉ 1 rue de la Légion d'Honneur, 93200 Saint-Denis ☎ 01 48 09 83 54
🕐 Apr–Sep Mon–Sat 10–6:15, Sun 12–6:15; Oct–Mar Mon–Sat 10–5:15, Sun 12–5:15 ✋ Moderate 🍴 Nearby (€) 🚇 Basilique Saint-Denis

CHANTILLY, CHÂTEAU DE

The Château de Chantilly houses the Musée Condé, named after one of the chateau's owners, the military hero Le Grand Condé. The 16th-century Petit Château contains the Princes' apartments and a library full of precious illuminated manuscripts; the Grand Château, destroyed during the Revolution and rebuilt at the end of the 19th century in Renaissance style, houses a magnificent collection of paintings by Raphael, Clouet, Ingres, Corot and Delacroix, as well as porcelain and jewellery. The luxurious 18th-century stables have been turned into the Musée Vivant du Cheval, illustrating the crafts, jobs and sports connected with horses.

www.domainedechantilly.com

✉ 40km (25 miles) north of Paris. BP 70243, 60631 Chantilly Cedex ☎ 03 44 27 31 80 🕐 Chateau, Musée Condé, park and gardens: Apr–Oct Wed–Sun 10–6 (park closes at 8), Nov–Mar Wed–Sun 10:30–5 (park closes at 6). Musée Vivant du Cheval: closed for renovation until 2012 ✋ Expensive 🍴 La Capitainerie (€), picnic tables in the park and Le Restaurant du Hameau (€€; tel: 03 44 57 46 21) 🚌 Free DUC shuttle bus from the station 🚇 RER D Châtelet-Les Halles to Chantilly-Gouvieux 🚆 Gare du Nord to Chantilly

DISNEYLAND® RESORT PARIS

Disneyland® Resort Paris offers fantasy, humour, *joie de vivre*, excitement and new attractions and rides every season. Besides Disneyland® Park and Walt Disney Studios® Park, there is a whole range of American-style hotels which offer special facilities.
www.disneylandparis.com

✉ 30km (19 miles) east of Paris at Marne-la-Vallée ☎ UK: 08448 008 898; in France: 0825 300 222 🕐 Varies with the season ✋ Expensive 🍴 Inside the park (€–€€€) 🚆 RER A Marne-la-Vallée/Chessy

FONTAINEBLEAU, CHÂTEAU DE

A fountain or spring, now in the Jardin Anglais, is at the origin of this splendid royal residence, which started out as a hunting pavilion at the heart of a vast forest. It was François I who made Fontainebleau into the beautiful palace it is today, although it was remodelled by successive monarchs. The imposing horseshoe staircase decorating the main facade was the scene of Napoleon I's moving farewell to his faithful guard in 1814. Beyond this building lies the Etang des Carpes (carp pool) with a pavilion in its centre, and farther on the formal French gardens. The oldest part of the palace, including the keep of the medieval castle, surrounds the Cour Ovale. The State Apartments contain paintings, furniture, the fine coffered ceiling of the Salle de Bal and frescoes in the Galerie François I.

www.musee-chateau-fontainebleau.fr

✉ 65km (40 miles) southeast of Paris. 77300 Fontainebleau ☎ 01 60 71 50 70 🕐 Wed–Sun 9:30–5 (Apr–Sep until 6pm). Closed 1 Jan, 1 May, 25 Dec ✋ Expensive 🍴 In the town nearby (€–€€€) 🚆 Gare de Lyon to Fontainebleau-Avon and 🚌 A or B ❓ Guided tour, shops

GIVERNY

Many art-lovers make a pilgrimage to the village of Giverny, about an hour's train ride from Paris, to see the house where the Impressionist Claude Monet lived, creating a flower-filled garden and a pond covered in waterlilies which he never seemed to tire of painting. Today, his home and garden are preserved and cared for by the **Fondation Claude Monet**. Nearby is the **Museum of Impressionism** which celebrates both his work and that of the artists who followed him to this place. To be inspired try one of the signposted footpaths that begin near the *mairie* (town hall).

✉ 80km (50 miles) west of Paris 🚉 Gare Saint-Lazare to Vernon then bus or taxi

ℹ Office de tourisme de Vernon-Pacy-Giverny, Maison du Temps Jadis, 36 rue Carnot, 27200 Vernon ☎ 02 32 51 39 60; www.cape-tourisme.fr

Fondation Claude Monet

✉ 84 rue Claude Monet, 27620 Giverny ☎ 02 32 51 28 21; www.fondation-monet.fr 🕐 Apr–Oct Tue–Sun 9:30–6 ✋ Inexpensive ❓ Bookshop

Musée des Impressionnismes

✉ 99 rue Claude Monet, 27620 Giverny ☎ 02 32 51 94 65; www.museedesimpressionnismesgiverny.com 🕐 Apr–Oct daily 10–6 (Jun–Sep Sat until10) ✋ Moderate, 1st Sun of the month free 🍴 Café (€) ❓ Bookshop

PARC ASTÉRIX

This theme park is based on the comic adventures of Astérix the Gaul and his companions, determined to resist Roman invaders. The story became famous through strip cartoons by Goscinny and Uderzo. Inside the park, you are invited to share Astérix's adventures in the Gauls' Village, the Roman Empire, Ancient Greece, and travel on the roller-coaster of the Great Lake.

www.parcasterix.fr

✉ 30km (19 miles) north of Paris. 60128 Plailly ☎ 0826 30 10 40 🕐 Early Apr–Aug daily 10–6 or 7 (mid-Jul to mid-Aug Sat until 11); Sep Sat–Sun 10–7; Oct Sat–Sun 10–6:30; last week Oct daily 10–6:30; last 2 weeks Dec daily 11–6:30 👋 Expensive 🍽 Several choices (€–€€) 🚌 Direct bus from 99 rue de Rivoli opposite Louvre: depart 8:45am, return 6pm from Parc Astérix, tel: 0826 30 10 40 🚆 RER B3 from Châtelet or Gare du Nord to Roissy Charles de Gaulle then shuttlebus every half hour ❓ Gift shops, picnic areas

SAINT-GERMAIN-EN-LAYE

The historic city clusters round its royal castle, favourite residence of Louis XIV. François I restored **Château Vieux** (Old Castle) and retained Saint-Louis's chapel and the 14th-century keep, now surmounted by a campanile. Le Nôtre designed the gardens and the Grande Terrasse. During the Sun King's stay, mansions were built around the castle for members of his court. Napoleon III restored the castle and turned it into the Musée des Antiquités Nationales, which houses archaeological collections.

www.saintgermainenlaye.fr

✉ 23km (14 miles) west of Paris

ℹ Maison Claude Debussy, 38 rue au Pain, 78100 Saint-Germain-en-Laye ☎ 01 34 51 05 12

Château de Saint-Germain-en-Laye

✉ Place Charles de Gaulle, 78105 Saint-Germain-en-Laye ☎ 01 39 10 13 00; www.musee-antiquitesnationales.fr 🕐 Wed–Sun 10–5:30; terrace daily summer 8am–9:30pm (winter until 5) 👋 Moderate, terrace free 🚆 RER A from Gare de Lyon to Saint-Germain-en-Laye

VAUX-LE-VICOMTE, CHÂTEAU DE

This architectural gem cost its owner, Nicolas Fouquet, his life. Fouquet had commissioned the best artists of his time: Le Vau for the building, Le Brun for the decoration and Le Nôtre for the gardens. Louis XIV did not take kindly to being outshone: Fouquet was arrested and imprisoned, while Louis commissioned the same artists to build him an even more splendid castle, Versailles.

The castle stands on a terrace overlooking magnificent gardens.

www.vaux-le-vicomte.com

✉ 55km (34 miles) southeast of Paris. Domaine de Vaux-le-Vicomte, 77950 Maincy ☎ 01 64 14 41 90 🕐 Jul–Aug daily 10–6; late Mar–May, Sep to mid-Nov Thu–Tue 10–6; mid–end Dec daily 11–6. Candelit visits Sat May–early Oct 8pm–12am with fireworks 1st and 3rd Sat of the month 10:30pm
💷 Expensive 🚃 Gare de Lyon to Melun then taxi or Châteauxbus shuttle Sat and Sun only

VERSAILLES, CHÂTEAU DE

The physical expression of a king's superego, Versailles turned out to be one of the most splendid castles in the world through the genius of the artists who built and decorated it. What began as a modest hunting lodge became the seat of government and political centre of France for more than a hundred years. A town grew up around the castle to accommodate the court. Several thousand men worked on the castle for 50 years, thousands of trees were transplanted, and 3,000 people could live in it.

The castle is huge (680m/2,230ft long) and it is impossible to see everything in the course of one visit. Aim for the first floor where the State Apartments are, including the famous Galerie des Glaces (Hall of Mirrors), as well as the apartments of the royal

couple, on either side of the marble courtyard. The north wing contains the Chapelle St-Louis built by Mansart and the Opéra, added by Gabriel.

The focal point of the park is the Bassin d'Apollon, a magnificent ornamental pool with a bronze sculpture in its centre representing Apollo's chariot coming out of the water. Two smaller castles, Le Grand Trianon and Le Petit Trianon, are also worth a visit, and Le Hameau, Marie-Antoinette's retreat, offers a delightful contrast.

www.chateauversailles.fr

✉ 20km (12.5 miles) southwest of Paris. 78000 Versailles ☎ 01 30 83 78 00

🕐 Château: Tue–Sun 9–5:30 (Apr–Oct until 6:30). Trianons: daily noon–5:30 (Apr–Oct until 6:30). Park: daily 8–6 (Apr–Oct until 8:30). Buildings closed 1 Jan, Easter Mon, 1 May, Whitsun, 1 Nov, 25 Dec

💷 Expensive; free 1st Sun of month Nov–Mar 🍴 Cafeteria (€) and restaurant (€€) 🚆 RER C Versailles-Rive Gauche

🚉 Gare St-Lazare to Versailles-Rive Droite

a drive

in and around the Forêt de Fontainebleau

The forest of Fontainebleau extends over a vast area along the left bank of the Seine, to the southeast of the capital.

Start at the Porte d'Orléans and follow the A6 motorway towards Evry and Lyon. Leave at the Fontainebleau exit and continue on the N37 for 7km (4 miles); turn right to Barbizon.

This village gave its name to a group of landscape painters who settled there in the mid-19th century. They were joined later by some of the future Impressionists: Renoir, Sisley and Monet. The **Auberge Ganne**, which they decorated with their paintings, is now a museum.

Leave Barbizon towards Fontainebleau.

Take time to visit the château (➤ 170), or at least the park, and to stroll around the town.

There are many ways to access the Route Ronde (D301) from the town – one is the N7, direction Bourron-Marlotte.

This scenic route takes you through the forest and offers many possibilities for walking and cycling.

Turn left on the D409 to Milly-la-Forêt.

This small town nestling round an imposing covered market is a traditional centre for growing medicinal plants. The Cyclop (1km/0.5 miles north) is a monumental modern sculpture which took 20 years to complete.

Take the D372 for 3.5km (2 miles); bear left to Courances.

The **Château de Courances** is set like a jewel in a magnificent park with pools, canals and small waterfalls.

Return to the main road and continue for 5km (3 miles), then rejoin the motorway back to Paris.

Distance 143km (89 miles)
Time 7–9 hours depending on length of visits
Start/end point Porte d'Orléans
Lunch Le Caveau des Ducs ✉ 24 rue Ferrare, 77300 Fontainebleau
☎ 01 64 22 05 05; www.caveaudesducs.com

Auberge Ganne
✉ 92 Grande Rue, 77630 Barbizon ☎ 01 60 66 22 27;
www.tourisme77.fr 🕐 Daily 10–12:30, 2–5:30 (Jul–Aug until 6);
closed 1 May and 24 Dec–2 Jan 🎫 Inexpensive

Château de Courances
✉ 91240 Milly-la-Forêt ☎ 01 40 62 07 71; www.courances.net
🕐 Chateau and park: Apr–Oct Sat, Sun and public hols 2–6:30; park
only: Wed 11:30–4:30 🎫 Moderate ❓ Guided tours

VINCENNES, CHÂTEAU DE

This austere castle, situated on the eastern outskirts of Paris, was a royal residence from the Middle Ages to the mid-17th century. Inside the defensive wall, there are in fact two castles: the 50m-high (164ft) keep (magnificently restored) built in the 14th century, which later held political prisoners, philosophers, soldiers, ministers and churchmen; and the two classical pavilions built by Le Vau for Cardinal Mazarin in 1654, Le Pavillon de la Reine, where Anne d'Autriche, mother of Louis XIV lived, and Le Pavillon du Roi, where Mazarin died in 1661. The Chapelle Royale, started by Saint-Louis and completed by François I, stands in the main courtyard.

www.vincennes.monuments-nationaux.fr

✉ 6km (4 miles) east of Paris. Avenue de Paris, 94300 Vincennes

☎ 01 43 28 15 48 🕐 May–Aug daily 10–6:15; Sep–Apr 10–5 :15. Closed 1 Jan, 1 May, 1 Nov, 11 Nov, 25 Dec ✋ Moderate 🚇 Château de Vincennes 🚌 46, 56 ❓ Guided tours, shops

HOTELS

CHANTILLY
Château de Montvillargenne (€€–€€€)
Large mansion in its own vast grounds, with covered swimming pool, sauna and sports facilities.
✉ 1 avenue François Mathet, 60270 Gouvieux ☎ 03 44 62 37 37; www.chateaudemontvillargenne.com 🚊 Gare du Nord to Chantilly-Gouvieux

DISNEYLAND® RESORT PARIS
Disney's Sequoia Lodge® (€€–€€€)
Each of the hotels of Disneyland® Resort Paris has its own authentic theme; this one recreates the rustic charm of a refuge in one of America's national parks.
☎ 01 60 45 51 00; www.hotelsdisneylandparis.fr 🚇 RER A Marne-la-Vallée/Chessy

FONTAINEBLEAU
Hôtel de l'Aigle Noir (€€€)
Napoleon III-style decoration for this air-conditioned hotel facing the castle. There is also a fitness club and indoor swimming pool.
✉ 27 place Napoléon Bonaparte, 77300 Fontainebleau ☎ 01 60 74 60 00; www.hotelaiglenoir.fr 🚊 Gare de Lyon to Fontainebleau-Avon

GIVERNY
Le Clos Fleuri (€)
Charming *chambre d'hôte* (B&B) close to the centre of the village, in a rustic building set in its own garden.
✉ 5 rue de la Dîme, 27620 Giverny ☎ 02 32 21 36 51; www.giverny-leclosfleuri.fr 🚊 Gare Saint-Lazare to Vernon then bus or taxi

PARC ASTÉRIX
Hôtel des Trois Hiboux (€)
Family-friendly lodge-style accommodation with bunk beds for children and a free shuttlebus to the theme park.
✉ Parc Astérix, 60128 Plailly ☎ 0826 30 10 40, www.parcasterix.fr 🚇 RER B3 from Châtelet or Gare du Nord to Roissy-Charles de Gaulle airport, then shuttlebus every half-hour, tel: 01 48 62 38 33

SAINT-GERMAIN-EN-LAYE
Pavillon Henri IV (€€–€€€)
Historic building near the famous Grande Terrasse; great views.
✉ 19–21 rue Thiers, 78100 Saint-Germain-en-Laye ☎ 01 39 10 15 15;
www.pavillonhenri4.fr 🚇 RER A Saint-Germain-en-Laye

VERSAILLES
Relais de Courlande (€€)
Attractive converted 16th-century farmhouse offering hydrotherapy.
✉ 23 rue de la Division Leclerc, 78350 Les Loges-en-Josas ☎ 01 30 83
84 00; www.relais-de-courlande.com 🚇 RER C to Versailles-Rive Gauche
🚆 Gare Saint-Lazare to Versailles-Rive Droite

RESTAURANTS

CHANTILLY
Château de la Tour (€€)
Refined cuisine and wood-panelling; terrace in summer.
✉ Chemin de la Chaussée, 60270 Gouvieux (1km/0.5 miles from Chantilly)
☎ 03 44 62 38 38; www.lechateaudelatour.fr 🕐 Lunch, dinner 🚆 Gare du
Nord to Chantilly-Gouvieux

FONTAINEBLEAU
L'Atrium (€–€€)
Pizzeria in the town centre; attractive year-round terrace dining.
✉ 20 rue France, 77300 Fontainebleau ☎ 01 64 22 18 36 🕐 Daily 11–11
🚆 Gare de Lyon to Fontainebleau-Avon then 🚌 A or B

GIVERNY
Restaurant Baudy (€)
Restaurant with rose garden, popular with Monet's disciples.
✉ 81 rue Claude Monet, 27620 Giverny ☎ 02 32 21 10 03 🕐 Apr–Oct 10–9:30

SAINT-GERMAIN-EN-LAYE
Ermitage des Loges (€€)
Reasonably priced cuisine with an emphasis on fish and seafood.
✉ 11 avenue des Loges, 78100 Saint-Germain-en-Laye ☎ 01 39 21 50 90;
www.ermitagedesloges 🕐 Lunch, dinner 🚇 RER A Saint-Germain-en-Laye

VAUX-LE-VICOMTE
La Mare au Diable (€€)
Lovely old 15th-century manor house with beams; terrace for summer meals.

✉ RN6, 77550 Melun-Sénart (10km/6 miles from Vaux-le-Vicomte)
☎ 01 64 10 20 90; www.lamareaudiable.fr 🕐 Lunch, dinner; closed Mon and Sun dinner 🚆 Gare de Lyon to Melun

VERSAILLES
Le Boeuf à la Mode (€)
Old-fashioned brasserie with sunny terrace serving excellent duck and vegetable spaghettis.

✉ Place du Marché, 4 rue au Pain, 78000 Versailles ☎ 01 39 50 31 99; www.restaurant-bistrot-traditionnel-versailles.com 🕐 Lunch, dinner 🚇 RER C to Versailles-Rive Gauche 🚆 Gare Saint-Lazare to Versailles-Rive Droite

SHOPPING

BARBIZON
Galerie d'Art Castiglione
One of many art galleries to be found in this popular artists' village.

✉ 21 Grande Rue, 77630 Barbizon ☎ 01 60 69 22 12 🚇 RER D to Melun, then taxi (5–10 min)

FONTAINEBLEAU
Boutique du Musée National de Fontainebleau
For history buffs fascinated by Napoleon I and European history at the beginning of the 19th century.

✉ Château de Fontainebleau, 77300 Fontainebleau ☎ 01 60 71 50 70 🚆 Gare de Lyon to Fontainebleau-Avon, then 🚌 A or B

SAINT-GERMAIN-EN-LAYE
Les Galeries de Saint-Germain
Close to the RER and the Château, more than 30 boutiques in les Galeries de Saint-Germain sell fashion, homeware and gifts.

✉ 13 rue de la Salle, 78100 Saint-Germain-en-Laye ☎ 01 39 73 70 67; www.cc-galeries.com 🕐 Mon–Sat 8:30–8, Sun 8:30–2 🚇 RER A Saint-Germain-en-Laye

VERSAILLES
Librairie-Boutique de l'Ancienne Comédie
This bookshop stocks 2,000 titles connected with the castle.

✉ Château de Versailles, passage des Princes, 78000 Versailles ☎ 01 30 97 70 98 🕐 May–Sep daily 9–6:30; Oct–Apr 9–5:30 🚇 RER C to Versailles-Rive Gauche 🚉 Gare Saint-Lazare to Versailles-Rive Droite

ENTERTAINMENT

CONCERT
Soirées Musicales au Château de Versailles
Concerts, mainly baroque music, in various venues in the palace, and at Bassin de Neptune for Grande Eaux Musicale (water music).

✉ Grille d'Honneur, Place d'Armes or Bassin de Neptune, 4 boulevard de la Reine, 78000 Versailles ☎ 01 30 83 78 89, www.chateauversaillesspectacles.fr 🕐 Vary but mainly Apr–Oct 💶 Moderate–expensive 🚌 171 🚉 Montparnasse to Versailles-Chantiers, St-Lazare to Versailles-Rive Droite or RER C to Versailles-Rive Gauche then for water music Phebus from stations to Bassin de Neptune

HORSE-RACING
Hippodrome de Chantilly
Flat racing Prix du Jockey-Club and Prix de Diane-Hermès in June.

✉ Route de l'Aigle, 60631 Chantilly ☎ 03 44 62 41 00; www.francegalop.com 🕐 Apr–Oct weekly 🚉 Gare du Nord to Chantilly-Gouvieux

SHOWS
Disneyland® Resort Paris
Buffalo Bill's Wild West Show
A fast moving dinner-show in the company of Buffalo Bill.

☎ Bookings: 01 60 45 71 00; www.disneylandparis.com 🕐 Daily 6:30 and 9:30

Vaux-le-Vicomte
Visites aux Chandelles
Tours of the Château de Vaux-le-Vicomte by candlelight take place every Saturday night from early May to mid-October.

✉ Château de Vaux-le-Vicomte, 77950 Maincy ☎ 01 64 14 41 90 🚉 Gare de Lyon to Melun then taxi or Châteauxbus shuttle Sat and Sun only

Sight locator index

This index relates to the maps on the covers. We have given map references to the main sights in the book. Some sights may not be plotted on the maps.

Index

Acknowledgements

The Automobile Association would like to thank the following photographers, companies and picture libraries for their assistance in the preparation of this book.

Abbreviations for the picture credits are as follows – (t) top; (b) bottom; (c) centre; (l) left; (r) right; (AA) AA World Travel Library.

4l Eiffel Tower, AA/B Reiger; **4c** Metro, AA/C Sawyer; **4r** Louvre, AA/J Tims; **5l** La Coupole, AA/B Reiger; **5c** Lafayette, AA/C Sawyer; **5r** Chateau de Fontainbleau, AA/M Jourdan; **6/7** Eiffel Tower, AA/B Reiger; **8/9** Musee d'Orsay, AA/M Jourdan; **10bl** Place de la Concorde, AA/K Paterson; **10br** old poster, AA/T Souter; **10/11** Boulevard St Michel, AA/C Sawyer; **11bl** Galerie Vivienne, AA/J Tims; **12bl** Croissant, AA/B Smith; **12br** Hediard and Fauchon, AA/T Souter; **13t** French bread, AA/C Sawyer; **13c** Jean-Paul Hevin chocolates, AA/C Sawyer; **13bl** market, AA/M Jourdan; **13br** Camomile flowers, AA/B Smith; **14/15** Jean-Paul Hevin chocolates, AA/C Sawyer; **14** market, AA/C Sawyer; **15bl** wine, AA/B Reiger; **15br** Montmartre, AA/M Jourdan; **16** Ile St-Louis, AA/M Jourdan; **17** Les Deux Magots cafe, AA/M Jourdan; **18** Brasserie Printemps, AA/K Blackwell; **19** Sacre Coeur, AA/T Souter; **20/21** Metro, AA/C Sawyer; **28/29** Bus, AA/M Jourdan; **30/31** Phonebox, AA/K Paterson; **34/35** Louvre, AA/ J Tims; **36/37** View from the Arc de Triomphe, AA/M Jourdan; **37** Arc de Triomphe, AA/K Blackwell; **38** Centre Georges Pompidou, AA/W Voysey; **39t** Centre Georges Pompidou, AA/T Souter; **39b** View from Centre Georges Pompidou, AA/J Tims; **40** Champs-Elysees, AA/K Blackwell; **40/41t** Laduree cafe, AA/K Blackwell; **40/41b** Champs-Elysees, AA/K Blackwell; **42** Les Invalides, AA/J Tims; **42/43** Les Invalides, AA/K Paterson; **44/45** Louvre, AA/M Jourdan; **46t** Musee d'Orsay, AA/M Jourdan; **46b** Musee d'Orsay, AA/M Jourdan; **46/47** Musee d'Orsay, AA/P Enticknap; **47** Musee d'Orsay, AA/M Jourdan; **48t** Notre Dame, AA/C Sawyer; **48b** Notre Dame, AA/C Sawyer; **48/49** Notre Dame, AA/C Sawyer; **49** Notre Dame, AA/T Souter; **50** River Seine, AA; **50/51** Iles St Louis, AA/C Sawyer; **52/53** Sacre Coeur, AA/T Souter; **53** Sacre Coeur, AA/K Paterson; **54** Eiffel Tower, AA/P Enticknap; **54/55** La Tour Eiffel, AA/J Tims; **56/57** Brasserie Printemps, AA/K Blackwell; **58/59** Cafe de Flore, AA/K Blackwell; **60/61** Buddha Bar, AA/C Sawyer; **62** La Coupole, AA/C Sawyer; **64/65** Eiffel Tower, AA/M Jourdan; **66/67** Jardin du Luxembourg, AA/M Jourdan; **68/69** The Seine, AA/K Blackwell; **70/71** Sainte-Chapelle, AA/K Blackwell; **72/73** Theatre des Champs Elysee, AA/B Reiger; **74/75** Musee Rodin, AA/M Jourdan; **76/77** Sacre Coeur, AA/P Enticknap; **78/79** Ritz hotel, AA/K Blackwell; **80/81** Galeries Lafayette, AA/K Paterson; **82/83** Lafayette shopping bag, AA/C Sawyer; **85** Cafe life, AA/K Paterson; **86** Bibliotheque Francois Mitterand, © JOHN KELLERMAN/Alamy; **87** Catacombes, Photolibrary; **88** La Conciergerie, AA/K Blackwell; **89** Institut du Monde Arabe, AA/M Jourdan; **90t** Musee Nacional du Moyan Age, AA/K Paterson; **90c** Musee de Cluny, AA/J Tims; **90/91** The Pantheon, AA/J Tims; **92** Jardin de Plantes, AA/T Souter; **93** Sainte-Chapelle, AA/J Tims; **94** River Seine, AA/M Jourdan; **101** Left Bank, AA/K Paterson; **102/103** Delacroix, museum, AA/J Tims; **104/105** Hotel Matignon, Photolibrary; **107** Musée du Quai Branly, AA/K Blackwell; **108** Rodin Museum, AA/M Jourdan; **110** Eglise de St-Sulpice, AA/M Jourdan; **117** Faubourg St-Honore, AA/C Sawyer; **118** Faubourg St-Honore, AA/C Sawyer; **119** Grand Palais, AA/M Jourdan; **120** Jardins des Tuileries, AA/M Jourdan; **122** Musee des Arts Decoratifs, AA/K Blackwell; **124** Musee Nissim de Camondo, AA/J Tims; **126** Cite de l'Architecture et du Patrimonie, AA/K Blackwell; **136** Opera Bastille, AA/K Blackwell; **136/137** Bibliotheque Nationale de France site Richelieu, AA/K Blackwell; **138l** Pere-Lachaise Cemetery, AA/K Blackwell; **138r** Pere-Lachaise, AA/K Blackwell; **139** Fauchon food store, AA/K Blackwell; **140t** Eglise St Eustache, AA/J Tims; **140b** Les Halles, AA/M Jourdan; **142/143** Museum Carnavalet, AA/K Paterson; **146t** Place des Vosges, AA/B Reiger; **146c** Place des Vosges, AA/K Paterson; **153** Montmartre, AA/M Jourdan; **154** Cimetiere de Montmartre, AA/K Blackwell; **154/155** Montmartre, © Anthony Wiles/Alamy; **156** Marche aux Puces de St-Ouen, AA/K Blackwell; **157** Montmartre Moulin de la Galette, AA/M Jourdan; **158** Romantic Life Museum, Photolibrary; **166/167** Chateau de Fontainbleau, AA/M Jourdan; **169** Chateau de Chantilly, AA/D Noble; **170** Chateau de Fontainbleau, AA/D Noble; **171** Giverny, AA/I Dawson; **172/173** Chateau de Vaux le Vicomte, AA/B Reiger; **174/175** Chateau de Versailles, AA/M Jourdan; **175t** Chateau de Versailles, AA/M Jourdan; **175b** Chateau de Versailles, AA/D Noble; **176** Foret de Fontainebleau, AA/D Noble; **178** Chateau de Vincennes/J Tims.

Every effort has been made to trace the copyright holders, and we apologise in advance for any accidental errors. We would be happy to apply the corrections in the following edition of this publication.

Street index

Keppler, Rue **6J**
Kléber, Avenue **6J**

Labat, Rue **4C**
Labie, Rue **5G**
Laborde, Rue de **11H**
Lacepède, Rue **25S**
Lacuée, Rue **28Q**
Laferrière, Rue **2E**
Laffitte, Rue **11H**
Lagille, Rue **1A**
Lagrange, Rue **24Q**
Lallier, Rue **3E**
Lamarck, Rue **1B**
Lamarck, Square **2B**
Lamartine, Rue **11H**
Lambert, Rue **4C**
Lamennais, Rue **7H**
Lauriston, Rue **5K**
Lavoisier, Rue **11H**
L Bourgeois, Allée **6M**
Léandre, Villa **2C**
Lecuyer, Rue **4C**
Ledru-Rollin, Avenue **28R**
Leibniz, Rue **1A**
Leibniz, Square **1A**
Lentonnet, Rue **4E**
Léon Jost, Rue **7G**
Léopold Bellan, Rue **15K**
Léopold-Sedar-Senghor, Passerelle **11L**
Lepic, Rue **2C**
Lhomond, Rue **24S**
Lille, Rue de **11L**
Linné, Rue **26S**
Lions Saint-Paul, Rue des **27Q**
Lisbonne, Rue de **9G**
Livingstone, Rue **4D**
Lobau, Rue de **25P**
Londres, Rue de **11G**
Longchamp, Rue de **5K**
Lord Byron, Rue **7H**
Louis le Grand, Rue **13J**
Louis Lépine, Place **24P**
Louvois, Rue de **13K**
Louvre, Place du **14M**
Louvre, Quai du **13M**
Louvre, Rue du **11L**
Lowendal, Avenue de **17Q**
L Philippe, Pont **25P**
Lubeck, Rue de **6K**
Lune, Rue de la **15J**
Lutèce, Rue de **24P**
Lyon, Rue de **28Q**
Lyonnais, Rue des **24T**

Mabillon, Rue **22Q**
Madame, Rue **22R**
Madeleine, Boulevard de la **11J**
Madeleine, Place de la **11J**
Magdebourg, Rue de **5L**
Magenta, Boulevard de **16G**
Mail, Rue du **14K**
Maine, Avenue du **20S**
Maine, Rue du **20T**
Malaquais, Quai **22N**
Malar, Rue **8L**

Malesherbes, Boulevard **11J**
Malus, Rue **25S**
Mansart, Rue **1D**
Manuel, Rue **3E**
Marbeuf, Rue **8J**
Marcadet, Rue **1B**
Marceau, Avenue **6J**
Marcel Proust, Allée **10K**
Marché Neuf, Quai du **24P**
Marché St-Honoré, Place du **12K**
Maréchal Gallieni, Avenue du **9M**
Margueritte, Rue **7G**
Marie, Pont **26Q**
Marignan, Rue de **8K**
Marigny, Avenue de **10J**
Mario Nikis, Rue **17R**
Martel, Rue **16H**
Martignac, Rue de **19N**
Martyrs, Rue des **3E**
Masseran, Rue **19R**
Mathurins, Rue des **12J**
Matignon, Avenue **9J**
Maubeuge, Rue de **4E**
Maurice de la Sizeranne, Rue **19R**
Max Hymans, Square **19T**
Mayet, Rue **19R**
Mazarine, Rue **23P**
Mazas, Voie **28R**
M Blanche, Impasse **1D**
Médicis, Rue de **23R**
Mégisserie, Quai de la **24N**
Messine, Avenue de **9H**
Midi, Cité du **2D**
Milan, Rue de **1E**
Milord, Impasse **1A**
Milton, Rue **3E**
Minimes, Rue des **27P**
Miollis, Rue **17R**
Mirbel, Rue de **25S**
Miromesnil, Rue de **10G**
Mogador, Rue de **12H**
Molière, Rue **13K**
Monceau, Rue de **8H**
Moncey, Rue **1E**
Moncey, Square **1E**
Mondovi, Rue de **11K**
Monge, Rue **25R**
Monnaie, Rue de la **14M**
Monsieur le Prince, Rue **23Q**
Monsieur, Rue **19Q**
Monsigny, Rue **13K**
Mont Cenis, Passage du **4A**
Mont Thabor, Rue du **11K**
Montaigne, Avenue **8K**
Montcalm, Rue **2B**
Montebello, Quai de **24Q**
Montholon, Rue de **15H**
Montmartre, Boulevard **14J**
Montmartre, Rue **14J**
Montorgueil, Rue **15K**
Montparnasse, Rue de **21S**
Montpensier, Rue de **13L**
Monttessuy, Rue de **7M**

Montyon, Rue de **14J**
Morland, Boulevard **27Q**
Morland, Pont **28R**
Mornay, Rue **27Q**
Motte-Picquet, Avenue de la **17Q**
Mouffetard, Rue **25S**
Muller, Rue **4C**
Murillo, Rue **8G**
M Utrillo, Rue **3C**

Naples, Rue de **10G**
Nations Unies, Avenue des **5L**
Navarin, Rue de **2E**
Navarre, Rue des **25S**
Neuf, Pont **23N**
Neuve Saint-Pierre, Rue **27P**
Néva, Rue de la **7G**
New York, Avenue de **6L**
Ney, Boulevard **1A**
Nicolas Houël, Rue **27S**
Nicolet, Rue **4C**
Norvins, Rue **2C**
Nôtre, Rue le **5M**
Notre-Dame de Lorette, Rue **2E**
Notre-Dame des Champs, Rue **21S**
Notre-Dame des Victoires, Rue **14K**
Notre-Dame, Pont **24P**

Observatoire, Avenue de l' **23S**
Odéon, Rue de l' **23Q**
Odessa, Rue d' **20S**
Opéra, Avenue de l' **13K**
Opéra, Place de l' **12J**
Ordener, Rue **2B**
Orfèvres, Quai des **23P**
Orléans, Galerie d' **13L**
Orléans, Quai d' **25Q**
Orléans, Square d' **2E**
Ornano, Square **4B**
Orsay, Quai d' **8L**
Orsel, Rue d' **3D**
Oslo, Rue d' **1B**
Oudinot, Rue **19Q**
Oudry, Rue **26T**
Ours, Rue aux **16L**

Paix, Rue de la **12J**
Palais, Boulevard du **24P**
Palatine, Rue **22Q**
P Albert, Rue **4C**
Palestro, Rue de **16K**
Panoramas, Passage des **14J**
Panthéon, Place du **24R**
Papillon, Rue **15H**
Paradis, Rue de **16H**
Parc Royal, Rue du **27N**
Pascal, Rue **25T**
Pasquier, Rue **11J**
Pasteur, Boulevard **18S**
Paul Barruel, Rue **17T**
Paul Baudry, Rue **8J**
Paul Feval, Rue **3C**

Paul Langevin, Square **25R**
Paul Valéry, Rue **5J**
Pavée, Rue **27P**
Payenne, Rue **27N**
P Deschanel, Allée **6M**
Penthièvre, Rue de **10J**
Pépinière, Rue de la **11H**
Percier, Avenue **9H**
Pereire Nord, Boulevard **5G**
Pereire Sud, Boulevard **5G**
Pérignon, Rue **18R**
Perle, Rue de la **27N**
Pernelle, Rue **25N**
Pérouse, Rue la **6J**
Pers, Impasse **4C**
P Escudier, Rue **1E**
Petites Ecuries, Rue des **16H**
Petit Musc, Rue du **27Q**
Petit, Pont **24Q**
Petits Carreaux, Rue des **15K**
Petits Champs, Rue des **13K**
Pétrelle, Rue **4E**
P Haret, Rue **1D**
Picard, Rue **4D**
Pierre 1er de Serbie, Avenue **7K**
Pierre Brossolette, Rue **24S**
Pierre Charron, Rue **7K**
Pierre Lafue, Place **21R**
Pierre Leroux, Rue **19Q**
Pierre Nicole, Rue **23T**
Pierre Sarrazin, Rue **23Q**
Pierre Sémard, Rue **4E**
Pigalle, Cité **2E**
Pillet-Will, Rue **13H**
Pirandello, Rue **26T**
Platanes, Villa des **2D**
P-L Courier, Rue **20P**
Point Show, Galerie **8J**
Poirier, Villa **17S**
Poissonnière, Boulevard **15J**
Poissonnière, Rue **15J**
Poissy, Rue de **25R**
Poitiers, Rue de **21N**
Pôle Nord, Rue du **2A**
Poliveau, Rue **26T**
Poncelet, Rue **7G**
Pont Neuf, Rue du **14M**
Ponthieu, Rue de **8J**
Pontoise, Rue de **25Q**
Portalis, Rue **10G**
Port-Royal, Boulevard de **23T**
Poteau, Passage du **2A**
Poulet, Rue **4C**
Poulletier, Rue **26Q**
Presbourg, Rue de **6J**
Président Wilson, Avenue du **5L**
Primevères, Impasse des **28N**
Procession, Rue de la **17T**
Prony, Rue de **8G**
Provence, Rue de **12H**
Pyramides, Rue des **13K**

190